Simply LOVE

4 Easy Strategies to Unlock your Child's Mind and Heart

Leanne Seniloli

To Josiah, Levi, Grace and Joseph Jnr.
You are my reason for life.
And to Joe, for your hope for the future.

A Letter from the Author

I was barely out of childhood myself, when I found out that I would soon be having a child of my own.

It was not what I had planned or pictured my life to be. At the time I discovered my pregnancy, I had my sights set on working my way to the top of the corporate world. Where I ended up was very, very different. But now, I would never change it, not for the world or even the most prominent corporate position.

The truth is, parenting didn't feel natural to me, and I never embarked on this journey in the way many had. My husband and I were married at 19 years old, a huge stretch from today's norm, and had our first baby at 20. This was the rude introduction to parenthood I received. Fresh out of study, living in a two-bedroom state house, and my husband continuing to study and working long shifts in a factory to provide. Our friends and the rest of society were light-years away from us, as they enjoyed their lives free from responsibilities, travelling, going out, and living it up. We embarked alone.

My home, the two-bedroom state house, was freezing, old, and sparse, furnished by the goodness of others, and complete with a baby that just wouldn't stop crying. Welcome to the life of parenting. My parenting life continued for many years like this, with the agony of poverty, disconnect from family and overwhelming feelings of despair, often bringing me to tears. However, it was these years that made me determined to learn and do all I can and be the absolute best mother I can be for my children.

My journey and experience as a mum has been the biggest learning curve I have ever undertaken. It has taught me more than any book, class, or course (and I am a nerd so I have done a lot of these)! It has been my greatest joy and pride, and yet also my greatest heart-wrenching ache.

The earliest years were the toughest, but looking back, they taught me the most. I was twenty-six years old, with four kids under the age of six, home-schooling the older two, and highly committed to Playcentre (a type of kindergarten run by parents) and volunteer work. I had a life that NONE of my peers did. I lived a large distance from family and had to learn how to do this parenting thing on my own. The pressure of these years brought me to breaking point many times, and our marriage has endured a cross-country road experience with bumps and potholes, hills and valleys.

Learning through this school of experience, I became purely focused on my children. They wouldn't be dependent on only what I had. I wanted them to remain starry-eyed, curious, and loving life. Though this was my goal, it has not always been achieved as I have wanted. I quickly learnt that money really can't buy everything. In fact, it buys very little of anything significant. It especially cannot buy a love and thirst for life. It rarely can buy the success we want for our children. And it cannot buy what their heart desires, which is true and pure unconditional love. This is the essence of life that we all long for. This is our privilege to give them and is completely in our power to do so.

This experience of mine is not without failure, though the teacher in me says there is no failure, only learning! So, I'll rephrase: this experience was not without many learning curves. This book is by no means a record of my magnificence. It may be the complete opposite. The tears when, as a one-year-old, my firstborn choked, and we scrambled to ring for an ambulance, or the tiredness of multiple hours at hospitals with many broken bones belonging to rambunctious boys. The despair and pain of constantly imparting lessons with little response, and the feeling that I had given everything. Sacrificed everything. Hoped for everything. And seen nothing from it—yet.

The joy and pride of sending my sons off as gentlemen to their first school ball nearly outshines it all. Or when my younger two children were chosen for the inter-school sports competitions, or each of them receiving multiple performing arts awards. But outside all of that is the day-to-day living of parenting. My story shares these experiences and highlights the researched principles, I have over time, applied in our lives. May they be a beacon of light for you too.

The time has flown by. I remember looking at teenage-sized clothes through unbelieving eyes, when my first son was just two and thinking that he will never be that big. He has now outgrown even those clothes!

I remember my second son always hanging off my leg, everywhere I went. Following me, smiling, and never letting me go. I now look up at him, lay my head on his 17-year-old chest and receive cuddles from his 6 ft. 3" frame.

What can I say to express this muddle of feelings? The absolute pride, the joy and the strength. And yet the tears, the ache, the pain, the separation. We give life, now we must defend it. We bear life and we pain. I grapple with this dichotomy; I try to understand what it takes to give your life for children and then bear the pain of separation. Yet this is the way of parenting life.

Here I am. By a miracle still standing. It is now 19 years from the day I painfully gave birth to my first son and a life entirely different from the one I had imagined. I have a marriage of 19 years (that is another long book!), and four children in total. I am still determined to be the best mother I can, and still learning how to do this the best way each day. I am now 39, one year away from the big 4-0 and I have four teenagers.

For parents of newborns, toddlers, primary, tweens, and teens; I am here with you and learning alongside you. I have learnt lessons. I have fought the battles and been enticed with the temptation of ease just as you have. What I try to keep in mind is the speed of time—just how fast they grow up.

Time goes much quicker than we can imagine, but it seems as if it will never pass when you are in the middle of nappies, milk, play-dates, washing and transporting. However, it will be gone before you know it.

I ask you, what do you want to remember? What do you want to look back on and say about these years with your children? What do you want them to remember?

Whatever you answer, know that your time is NOW. You are writing that story and making that history. The reality is you will rarely remember the tiredness, the cleaning, or how dirty your hair or shirt was for all those years. But you will remember that you gave them your all. You remember the moments you were with them. And when you look back, your chest will swell with gratitude, and regret will be only a concept, one that does not belong to you.

May you find comfort, solace and advice within these pages that change your future for the better. That is my hope for all.

Leanne

The Vision for L.O.V.E.

#thenaturalchildhoodmovement

Modern day parenting just seems difficult. With a million programmes and philosophies, globalisation and information overload, it can be tough just to find out the basics. What really matters? How can I give my child the best start? What are the keys to success?

If you have ever felt that you have done all you can for your kids, or you want to do your best as a parent, then this book is for you. My intention in creating this book is that through sharing my lessons, you and your children will benefit. That you can avoid the mistakes I have made. So that your kids will flourish and enjoy the best you, and so that you as a parent, can love your role as mum or dad. And so that you all can make the most of the beautiful journey which is family.

As parents we love our children and want the best for them. As you are reading this book, it's probably safe to assume that you are one of those parents. Our instinct is to protect, nurture and care for our young. Then why can the parenting journey be so challenging? Why do these relationships sometimes break down, leaving us disappointed and unfulfilled? Why are many of us feeling like we are ready to give in and to give up?

What is it about the way that we are doing parenting now that heaps the pressure on both parents and children? Often our expectations and hopes for our family are unrealised because we just don't know how to raise our children effectively. Add onto that the busyness of modern life and the distractions of the internet and modern gadgets, our lives are filled to overflowing.

In this book you will find four easy principles that you can apply to your parenting today. You will discover a real-life story of parenting that understands exactly where you are, and will inspire you, because honestly, if I can do it, you definitely can too!

In these pages we will have a conversation about children and family, and all the joy and struggle that they bring. It is the purpose of this book to equip you with strategies so that you can give your child the best opportunities in life. It is not a cookie cutter model, but a method that allows you to still be you while you implement these researched and powerful principles.

It is my hope that when you finish this book you will be confident in your abilities as a parent and truly feel that your parenting is a great and important work. You are creating opportunities for your family, and I want you to understand your immense value in their lives.

You will be able to see a way to return to simple parenting principles that build up and encourage healthy child development. In doing so, it is my wish that you will find your heart once again being filled with gratitude and the contentment of parenting, and that your parenting becomes your pride and joy.

Overall, these pages remind us to take up our position as parents and wholeheartedly accept the role given to us, not to simply just do the job, but to journey in L.O.V.E. and be empowered with ways to love the entire journey.

I have summed up the four principles of parenting success into the acronym of L.O.V.E:

L = Language

O = Outdoors

V = Vestibular Stimulation (movement)

E = Exploration

It is from my own experience raising my four children with my husband of 19 years, my training as an early childhood teacher and neuro developmental therapist that I write this approach to parenting. My hope is that it inspires, informs and ignites a passion within you to be the best parent you can be. This isn't a rule book; it's a guide, a philosophical standing and a list of discoveries, written in the hope that you can learn from my failings and education. Together we can change the course of generations. May these stories, lessons and learnings encourage you to be all you can, for you and your children.

My intention is that you will discover ways to help combat disconnect. To parent on purpose and to love wholeheartedly. If we see love as more than a fuzzy feeling, we begin to understand the paramount importance of our role in this world. Our love is there when our children are at their worst, so that they get to know unconditional acceptance. The L.O.V.E principles are organic and holistic building blocks of nurturing children to grow families closer together.

When we have L.O.V.E we have a healthy, productive and secure foundation for childhood. Our children can grow and become all they can be, reaching their fullest potential and maturing into contributing members of society. This book is a means for personal reflection and purposeful action. Action that is grounded in identity of self, culture, and community.

The four principles of L.O.V.E are in no way conclusive of all we need to do as parents, but they are an excellent place to start. Language, Outdoors, Vestibular Stimulation and Exploration allow connection and holistic development of the whole child. It gives us a path to follow as we release children's fullest potential.

In many ways, raising children is like raising a flourishing garden. The time, the effort, the patience. My own garden certainly reflects the work gone into it. Our homemade, ill-shaped compost box keeps us supplied with year-long spoils to feed our garden. We have some plants that were already strong and healthy when we bought them, and then we have our 'babies' that we have raised from seedlings.

It's easy, theoretically. Seed. Time. Care. Harvest. Of course, with a few techniques and a little knowledge, and unwavering commitment anyone can grow a garden. By planting the seeds, we will see a harvest in time.

My garden is flourishing, so much so that I can barely take credit for it. I mean, in some ways I can. But in many others, I can't. I did not cause the plant to grow, I just provided the environment.

And in this illustration is a profound truth of parenting. We plant. We water. We fertilise. But we do not determine the crop. We sow. We reap. We strive to find the best soil and we plant our creation of organic quality. It is raised amongst plants of like kind. And each plant is given the environment it needs to thrive. But that is where our influence ends. We do our best. We do our part. Job done. Our role is one of environment and nurture.

It isn't always an easy job. The path is fraught with potholes, hills and valleys.

But the best path is often the one least travelled.

So, travel with me my companion, may you find your path forward.

Contents

What does every child need?

L.O.V.E

L·O·V·E

Language

L

Language

Language, n. the method of human communication, either spoken or written, consisting of the use of words in a structured and conventional way.

> **Language** unlocks and enables communication and emotional intelligence; verbal and non-verbal communication, written or oral; expressiveness; external demonstration of internal processes; eloquence; understanding; connection with others; and a foundation for all learning.

When I think of talking to my children, two memories jump out at me. The first was when I had just given birth to my first son. It wasn't a difficult delivery in comparison to many, but no one really prepares you for that experience, do they?

After many hours of delivering this child into the world, this child around whom my whole life will now centre, I couldn't believe what I was looking at. The tiniest of fingers and fingernails, the button nose and eyes that tried to open, the mop of dark hair on his head and his frail body. I remember the pain, the shaking, the sights and sounds as if all my senses were on high alert. And from this place, without any previous thought of what I would do after he was born, I reached for him. I snatched him from the midwife and clung to him and proceeded to whisper reassuring words. 'Don't worry, mummy's here, shhhh, I love you, shhhh, it's okay...', as he cried his first breaths of life.

My husband stood there, staring, too scared to touch him, afraid he would break his tiny body with his huge hands. He could barely comprehend the scene before him. But even so, as soon as I passed our first boy into his arms, he instinctively began to talk to him too. Greeting him and reassuring him that daddy was there too.

The sight of our child, after waiting 9 months to see him, just pulled that response straight out of us. No one gave us a script or told us the first three things to do with a child. But as soon as we held that boy in our arms our words flowed. They expressed our love, our longing to see him and the awe that we finally were.

After my husband left for the night I lay there with my son, staring and whispering, touching and talking long into the night. In awe of what had just occurred and unable to fully put into words the magic of the moment (yet whispering and writing and communicating the experience nonetheless).

Another prominent memory I have when I think of talking to my children is nowhere near as glamorous and is quite painful to remember.

'Just shut up, sit down, and do your work. Stop being stupid! If you don't do this, you'll end up dumb,' I yelled at one of my boys several years later. The words were harsh, and my tone was harsher. I regretted them immediately, and despite my boiling anger I knew what I said was wrong. He did what I told him, but the look of hurt on his face is one I'll never forget. He was asking for help and because he still didn't understand how I was explaining something to him, I exploded. Words I can never take back. I'm sure many of you can relate.

Whether it is words of love or words of anger, our words have such tremendous power. They can inspire, encourage and esteem both ourselves and others, or they can destroy, degrade and deplete. Whatever way we use them, they wield power. Yet despite their importance they are also natural to us. Language and communication is something we learn from the moment we are born, and something many of us try to perfect throughout our lifetime. With words, our tone, our body language and our written words, we are communicating all the time. Even without knowing it, we are refining the way we communicate and teaching our children how to do so.

In this section on language we will be looking at three main areas. **Spoken language, body language** and **written communication**, and their importance in our children's lives. We will touch on ways that we can help our children develop their language, how we can know verbal and written languages as well as love languages, and ways in which we can reflect on specific areas of change.

When thinking about language what comes to mind for your family? How do you use language? How do your children use language?

Language is connection. Whether positive or negative, we make connections to others through our use of language. It is the process of sharing oneself and one's life with another.

Spoken or oral communication has been present in societies much longer than written communication, and even though both are important, there is no mistaking the physicality of talking with another person, looking in their eyes and feeling connected. This is why, for centuries, groups of people would meet, passing down stories of ancestors and generations around a campfire. Our language taught others, directed others, and shared a piece of who we were.

When we are talking to someone face to face, we learn how to read facial expressions and body language, and then use our knowledge instinctively to understand others. Children subconsciously pick up on this and this is exactly what they need to do in their early years.

Let's think of children aged 0-3. When we are talking to them we do a lot more than just teach words and the structure of sentences. We communicate who we are, and they see who they are through our communication. This face to face language is needed as much as possible with young children. It defines them, and shows them how to use words, tone, inflection, and a whole heap of other things. Face to face spoken language is extremely important, and preferable to anything digital— especially cartoons!

'Language is connection. Whether positive or negative, we are making a connection'.

The Languages of Love

It is my premise that everything we do for our children is birthed out of love. Of course, there are many things in this world that cause us to doubt this, but overall, we love our children and we want to do our best for them. This is often much to our despair! Yet, often as they grow up there are major feelings of disconnection, isolation and at times our children will still feel unloved. Why is this? How can we help our children know deep down in their soul that they are unconditionally loved? How can we deeply and permanently validate their being, their purpose and sense of self-worth?

Chapman and Campbell (1997) show us that there are many ways of giving and receiving love in their book The 5 Love Languages. This book tells us that when we understand how our children give and receive love, then we can ensure we are showing them love in a way that is most meaningful to them. These languages are: Quality Time, Acts of Service, Physical Touch, Words of Affirmation and Gifts. Often, we tend to give love one way and enjoy receiving it another.

Imagine you walked into a room and everyone was speaking a foreign language. How would this experience feel? Could we even guess what they are saying? Probably not. This is the same with love. We have to learn what resonates most with our children, how it feels to them as opposed to how it feels to us.

For example, I am not much of a 'Physical Touch' person. Someone who appreciates the language of touch will always be standing right next to you, enjoy holding hands, be wanting hugs and invading your personal space bubble! To me, this is okay every now and then, but I need my space. It just so happens that one of my kids loves it! This is the child who was constantly hanging off my leg as a toddler. I couldn't go anywhere without this little cutie clinging on to me and smiling up at me. It filled his tank! But as for mine, errrr...

Through the years he has continued to be the same. He is the first to kiss us good morning and the last to grab a hug, and then one last hug before bed. Even as a teen, taller than me, we still find him clambering onto my knee in the evening for a cuddle! It's quite an amusing sight and we often wonder just how long it will last. But he just loves it. It does something deep in his soul that recharges him. But me—nope. I have had to learn to stop what I am doing and pay attention to him in this way because if I didn't, he would feel as if I had rejected him, and instead of filling him up, it would be a major withdrawal.

Understanding this concept, that we all receive love differently, is essential in parenting. If you have more than one child, you know how different they are. When we learn how to love them the way they need, it improves our relationship with them, their trust in us, and subsequently their behaviour.

Most importantly, it allows us to feel the love, acceptance and joy of being family. We are communicating using each other's languages and can really feel the love that we have always been trying to give.

Developing Language

It is said that by age two a child should be able to know and speak between 50 and 200 words and will be starting to create two-word sentences (Childtalk, 2011). But how do they do this?

Children are not born communicating with words. They simply operate through primitive reflex movement patterns. However, within 24 months they are forming complex sentences and demonstrating thinking capacities. This is an amazing feat.

What occurs in this time period to allow such tremendous growth? Are there things we can do to increase our children's intelligence at this time? Or is their development and intelligence set in stone? And how important is language, really?

Huge questions, I know, especially as a parent. And what is our role as parents in this? Are we the task masters forcing our children to achieve? Or are we the passive 'she will get there eventually' supporters? Do we have a role in language at all, or is that the job of the teacher? Questions I am sure you have all asked at some stage.

It can be complicated to grapple with the big questions, and there is so much information out there telling us what to do or not do that it can get very confusing. Overall, I think we need to ask, is there any standard 'right' way of doing things?

It is good to realise that language doesn't have to be hard, especially in the early years. The child's mind is like a sponge literally a sponge that soaks everything up. Well, this can work for you or against you, but it's good to know they have a huge amount of curiosity and eagerness to learn and discover. Just the common everyday normal interactions we have with our child give us the opportunity to expand their vocabulary and their long-term capacity. It is in these simple interactions when we eat, play, walk, and drive that we are mirroring, forming attachment, modelling and demonstrating. Unsure what this means? Don't worry, I'll explain this more.

If you are reading this book, it is probably safe to assume you have children or work closely with children. In line with this, let's remember back to the first time you held a newborn baby. I suspect the natural thing for you to do was to affectionately touch them, look them in the eye and smile at them. You most probably proceeded to pull silly faces, with eyebrows raised and a goofy grin on your face. You then would have attempted 'baby speak'. You know, that's the, 'Aren't you a little cutie? Yes, you are! You're such a good girl', babble that we do to babies who can't communicate. Or maybe you recall interacting with a child who was at the 'bababa dada' stage and you imitated them enthusiastically. Perhaps you sat enraptured as a young child rattled off imaginary stories of villains and victors and you kindly reiterated their words, joining in the story.

These seemingly natural interactions, which we barely think about and very young children cannot fully understand, are providing the basis of language. When that child sees your facial expressions, hears the tone of your voice and feels the physical connection, they are learning language. They are learning the foundations of communication, even if they cannot respond to you, they are beginning to understand your message if not your words. This all adds to their pool of knowledge—developing the language centres of the brain, who they are and who they see themselves as.

When we repeat sounds and naturally demonstrate how our voices rise and fall with words in sentences, we model how to speak, and the child develops language abilities. This is why we must talk and talk and talk to our children. They hear the tone of your voice and learn that by making sounds—even if

This wee darling is mirroring the parents' facial expressions and emotional response.

not the right sound—they can communicate. This is especially great when you want them to stop crying and screaming at you! This process is called mirroring, and it is how the child gains an image of themselves as well as develops their language. It is like a mental mirror which creates an image in their mind of who they are and who we are.

'When we repeat sounds and naturally demonstrate how our voices rise and fall with words in sentences we model how to speak, and the child develops language abilities. This is why we must talk and talk and talk to our children'.

Mirroring has been proven by research to be extremely important for young children (Rayson et al, 2017), impacting their thinking and behaviour well into adulthood. However it is not always easy to get this right when they become teenagers with their own thoughts and ideas. Kolvs (1998) explains that there are strategies to help the process of mirroring in older children:

1. Step back emotionally

2. Reflect

3. Ask 'did I get it?' Do I understand what they are trying to communicate with me?

4. Ask 'is there more?' Do I need further understanding to communicate effectively with this child?

These can ensure that your child feels that their feelings have been heard. In honesty, this has been very hard for us, being raised in the 'do what I tell you' generation, and at times I have heard that phrase coming out of my mouth too. Yet in the spirit of learning, we are all on the same path of improvement, and this strategy helps us too. When our children are going through things that they don't know how to process and they want to talk to us, it is a privilege as much as it can feel a frustration. We need to remember that it is not about us and our emotions, but about their feelings and helping them learn to understand them. This can be particularly hard for busy parents like us who are constantly on the go. But it is worth the effort of investment, even if we don't get it right the first time.

During the first three years, children are gradually forming a mental image of themselves. What the child sees on our face, they will see in their mind. Therefore, whatever interpretation the child makes from our words and actions becomes their sense of self. If we show them facial expressions that communicate that they are loved, clever and accepted then this is what they will believe. However, the opposite is also true. If we show them through our facial expressions that we are mad, unhappy with them or not paying attention to them then they will grow to believe that they are not worthy of love and acceptance and are therefore rejected. What the child interprets we are saying becomes who they think they are. It becomes their sense of self – their self-esteem. It really can't be said enough just how important this process is. This is why face to face communication will forever outweigh anything you can buy for your child or allow them to watch.

Who would have thought so much could be gained from such 'babble?'

If you know a child that is not developing language in line with their developmental milestones, it is important to look for the reasons why in order to offer the best support. All children do develop at different rates, but developmental milestones are important. Here are some guidelines:

4 – 6 months old:

The child engages in vocal play and babble sounds.

7 – 12 months:

They use babbling consonant-vowel combinations. They play with intonation and sound combinations which begin to sound similar to familiar words.

12 – 24 months:

They child points to objects you name and makes gestures and recognizes their name. Uses single words and has more than 20 words by 18 months. They will imitate noises.

2 – 3 years:

The child uses between 100 – 200 words. They understand simple questions and directions. They use more and more words each week.

3 – 4 years:

Uses approximately 1000 words. Speaks in 4 – 6 word sentences. Starts to tell stories. Speaks clearly enough for other people to understand them. At this stage they should also be able to follow 3 consecutive instructions.

If a child from the ages of 2-3 is preferring to use gestures rather than language, uses an unusual tone of voice, and can't follow simple directions, it is important to consult a professional. Imagine how that child's world feels without any language to express themselves. It gives us a glimpse of why children have many emotional and social problems and outbursts when their language isn't fully developed, why there is extreme frustration and consequent misbehaviour. Life would feel hard, out of control and exhausting.

Some causes of language development complications can be due to primitive (baby) reflexes still being present, developmental delay in other areas, or physical anatomy problems such as being tongue-tie or having underdeveloped muscles.

Language is extremely important. If a child is delayed in this area it will lead to isolation and much frustration later. When they are not able to communicate thoughts and feelings it can become lonely and exasperating to be unable to share their inner self. Couple this with the self-consciousness about how they may be different from other children, and it leaves the child on an uneven playing field. Imagine having many thoughts and ideas but not knowing how to express them!

Thankfully there are a range of different services that we can now access to help our children with speaking. These include:

- Doctors
- Speech and language therapists
- Special education workers

- Teachers
- Reflex remediation programmes (such as the INPP method provided by Without Limits Learning)

How can we help our children develop as much language as possible? The simplest way is to incorporate it into daily routines. That means talk! Tasks such as changing a nappy can provide a great opportunity for language development. When we talk and explain what is happening and calmly interact with the child, they are learning to trust that you are there to meet their needs and care for them. This is the beginning of any language development: a relationship with the person they are talking to! And this is even more important with children who are shy, withdrawn or aware of their shortcomings with speech. When children are little, we can't underestimate the power of our connection with them, and even though we may think it is babbling to babies, it is forming amazing connections in their brains. The much-needed attachment connections that support all development. It is in these simple routines that we form a deeper relationship, trust and attachment with the child and model language to them. Therefore, it is attachment that initiates language. From strong attachments and positive language can flow natural positive relationships, and from there our children learn to speak the words of our language that communicate their thoughts and, eventually, feelings.

The Language of Attachment

It really cannot be emphasised enough that attachment is the biggest contributor to a child's successful development. What is attachment and how do we develop it? The good news is that most of the time it is something that occurs naturally between a baby and their primary caregiver. However, if this isn't the case for you, THAT'S OKAY!

This isn't about heavy-handed judgement, but instead ways of connecting and developing all aspects of our child's development. If attachment has been slow, the first thing to do would be to talk to your family doctor. Second to that, surround yourself with people who can support you and your baby. From family, to religious and community organisations, there are a lot of wonderful people doing amazing work to support those who need it.

The best place for a baby to be is with their primary caregiver. It is as essential as oxygen. They need and must have close physical contact with you and then the broadening and deepening of a genuine relationship. Just love them. It's not an exact science. If you love someone, what do you do? How do you want to be? Close, smiley, joyful, relaxed? All of those things. Relax a little and be with them naturally. Give them your time and heartfelt devotion.

If you are struggling with attaching to your baby, don't allow guilt to rule you. Each and every one of us is unique in how we think and feel about our children. However, if you feel you need some support, I encourage you to take action on it. You are of paramount importance to your child. One in a million. You matter. Do it for yourself and your baby will benefit from it also.

It is important to connect with your baby as soon as possible. From the moment they are born they are learning about how to interact with others, and their place and role in the world. A newborn baby's natural instinct is to connect with their primary caregiver, and most often that is Mum.

There are videos of newborn babies being placed on their mother's stomach just after birth. These little beings, using only the survival instinct of primitive reflexes, initiate the plantar reflex which causes a stepping motion. As the babies push their feet into their mothers' stomachs, they slowly and painstakingly 'crawl' up the torso until they find the breast. This is without any intervention or help from adults. They make it all the way up and then utilise the rooting reflex to find the breast to start feeding. Gradually developing the suck reflex to feed. This is such an amazing display of the natural drive we have for survival and connection. Ingrained in us from the moment of conception. The image of mum and baby chest to chest, connected in this close intimacy, is a miracle. Where some other animals eat their young, our drive is to nurture and protect.

'Positive attachment needs to be formed within the first few days of life and continue through into adulthood'.

It is from this natural connection that our attachments and language grow, and our children's whole development can be stunted from a lack of it. Lack of attachment to a caring loving figure in the early years of life has been linked to many cases of children's behavioural and academic problems at school, and teens' social problems later in life. If a child does not gain this attachment, it can lead to childhood depression, anger, misbehaviour and low self-esteem. At its worst, it can lead to involvement in crime and other things that we really don't want for our children. I know you don't want that any more than I do – because you are reading this book!

So, what is attachment? Attachment is the deep and enduring bond that connects one person to another. It is essential for healthy emotional and social development. Think of your mum or dad, or whoever raised you. You may not remember your earliest experiences as a young child, but you will have a sense or a feeling about those years.

In fact, research is again proving that all these memories are stored in our brain and body even if we don't consciously remember them (Leaf, 2018). There may be a particular thing you love to do such as read a book, sit closely talking to someone, or walk in the bush with a close friend, and it will bring back feelings of joy. It reminds you of a close connection with someone special, and quality time and communication being shared. It is a feeling of knowing you are cared for, loved and accepted unconditionally. A feeling that you have a place in this world, you are meant to be here and the fact that you are here is important. This is attachment. A strong love. Security. Value in being.

Positive attachment needs to be formed within the first few days of life and continue through into adulthood. But in essence, the earliest years are the most vital as the brain is developing fastest in this period. This is just one reason why our role as parents and caregivers is important—there really is no one who can take your place in your child's life! Your value to your children is immeasurable.

You will see how easy it is to develop a lifestyle and a way of living and growing which increases the connection between you and your children when you are intentional about it. When you begin to focus on connections and communication, I am positive you will begin to enjoy your children more and dream of what your family can be. Quite simply, it is love. A practical action of an inner feeling. Communication and connection provides a space where children can rise to their own ultimate potential in the context of a safe, loving and accepting relationship.

As your love and attachment to your child gets stronger and stronger, words will naturally flow from you. This is the

Even when they are tweens and teens they still love a reason to stay in bed longer and snuggle up to you. Enjoy!

beginning of language development, and from this relationship your language will change and grow and deepen as your connection to your child does. Language is both influenced by, and influences attachment. Spend time, talk, grow together and your child's language will develop. This language will spur important growth in your child's brain and will provide the platform for further learning and development.

Barriers to Language

If language is supposed to be a natural process, why are many children not developing the needed skills? I believe that one of the biggest reasons for this is our modern day living. The blessing and curse of technology. Don't get me wrong, I am not a technophobe and my kids have devices, and yes more than one each, but it can be a very real and dangerous parenting trap.

As an educator I have seen a lot of toddlers and pre-schoolers walking into the centre while on a cell phone or device. I have seen parents pull it out the minute they come to pick up their child because their child screams for it, and it is their way of keeping them quiet. I have seen children talk like cartoon characters because the most language input they were getting was from cartoon programmes. I have seen New Zealand children talk with an American accent because the TV talks to them more than people do. I have seen exhausted parents' hand over the 'educator' or 'babysitter', and yes, I can totally sympathise with the feeling of exhaustion, but our children are now suffering real problems because of the overuse of electronic devices.

I often see families sitting at a restaurant waiting for their dinner, and every member of the family is on a device, from Mum and Dad, to the teen, the primary-school-aged child, and the three-year-old! What is happening to us? What are we doing? Why do we squash our natural inclination for connection and community with a fake version through a screen? When did we begin to think that having our eyes glued to a screen was better for us than talking to the family around us? Do we really take measure of how much time we allow our children on screens?

I would like to say that these are extreme examples, but unfortunately, they are not. It's devastating that our family relationships are breaking down, and that people are finding more joy and affirmation from a TV show, a YouTube channel, or Instagram than their own family. For young children this is even more devastating.

The research is now coming out about the impact of technology on our physical or social-emotional development, and what is being discovered is disturbing. Researchers have found that the part of the brain stimulated when someone is playing a video game is the same part of the brain that is stimulated with substances such as heroin—it's addictive. This means that video games are just as addictive as drugs and smoking (Bauerlein, 2009).

Now we wouldn't give our children a smoke, would we? We also know that overexposure to violent games and programmes causes more of a tendency to act violently later in life, so why do we do it? The reality that we are just not facing as a society is that technology is changing our brains—and not for the better. It is making us lazy, outsourcing our thinking capacities to computers, rewarding us for the use of technology and creating a desire to constantly be attached to it. It hinders the development of intimacy, trust and empathy and impacts our ability to form meaningful relationships (Leaf, 2018). Technology must have boundaries in our children's lives if we want them to succeed in all areas.

Children's eyes, brains and bodies are developing at such a huge rate that they take in everything. We don't fully know how constant screen time will affect eyesight 20 or 40 years down the road. We want to give our children the best. They want these things, their friends have these things, and we want them to fit in. However, the BEST thing a parent can do is simply be with the child, and if they can't, then ensure someone who unconditionally loves them can. Give them time, and attention, and genuine interest. It is much more effective than a phone, a tablet or a video game.

How will our children learn how to communicate properly and effectively if there is no one there to show them? This is both our privilege and responsibility as parents, and this work we do in our children's lives at a young age will have a reward later in life for everyone.

Another barrier to the development of language is busyness. We have the most technology, money, and support systems than anyone else in any period of history, yet we are the busiest. Rushed off our feet, exhausted, and stressed. Something is going wrong here as our children are living the same kind of lives, and it is negatively affecting their development.

'If we are overscheduled, we are not teaching our children how to rest and there is no time for natural relationships to flourish'.

I understand the pressure modern life places on us. Well and truly. Even as I write this, my calendar is packed with work responsibilities, children's schooling, after school activities, family obligations, and all sorts of things that are supposed to be 'good' to do. Just for example's sake, here is this week in the Seniloli house:

Me – lecturing, relieving in a preschool, running a business, book writing, study, dropping kids off, picking kids up, and yes, all the house responsibilities (cooking, cleaning, never-ending washing!!);

My husband – full time work, part time musician, dropping kids off, picking kids up, extended family responsibilities;

Eldest – school NCEA, dance crew four times per week, physical training once a week, job hunting, studying for driver's license, youth group, band practice, house chores;

Second child – school NCEA level 1 exam prep, youth group, band practice, sports trips at school, teacher meetings, losing all his stuff and trying to find it, house chores;

Third child – school, homework, art class, youth group, house chores;

Fourth child – school, homework, touch rugby trip, basketball practice, youth group, organising his social life because friends are always full of drama at this age, house chores.

Therefore, I completely understand just how busy life can be! Often this leaves no time for friends, relaxation, or just plain old fun. The balance of this really is up to the individual and the priorities of the family, as there is no perfect, one-size-fits-all family model. However, I do know that your physical and mental state will quickly let you know if you are trying to squeeze too much into your days and weeks, and the same is true for our children. I have learnt this lesson the hard way. If we are overscheduled, we are not teaching our children how to rest and there is no time for natural relationships to flourish.

I have been actively considering our busyness as a family in more recent years, and more often saying no to things that will put more pressure on the kids or take away from family time. I remember reading books when my older two were just toddlers, and they would give advice like, 'make sure you have at least one night a week where you are all home as a family and can enjoy time together'.

I used to think 'I can't wait for the day when I can just have one night off from my kids!' I totally understand the claustrophobic feeling of constantly being surrounded by messy kids who need attention. However, in spite of it, I will give the same advice those books gave me. Make sure, at least once a week, you have time all together as a family. This is still just as essential when the children are teenagers as it is when they are toddlers. They may fight you, not understand, and argue. But at the end of the day they will eventually love and appreciate all your efforts to keep your family close.

Time together with teenagers is key for their language development and communication. The discussions we have together in these times aren't planned or prepared for, but they are essential for real life. Ethical questions about animal testing, practical questions about driving cars, emotional questions about friends' betrayals, it goes on and on. Our children don't want to talk to us as much when they are older, but if we provide the time and safe space for them to do so they will. Be prepared that it is often the time when you don't really want to, or you are the busiest. However, if you have a conscious effort to connect with them at these times you will deepen the relationship and trust between the both of you.

One way I try to help overcome the busyness is to have a delicious meal together in the school holidays before the term starts and talk about the goals and outcomes that everyone wants to achieve—including Mum and Dad. This way the children are deciding what is important to them and we are deciding what we can commit to. We share this together so that we have each other's support. They all need to identify what they will need to overcome to meet these goals, and what support they will need. We even decide on a reward at the end of the term if they achieve their goals. This way we are all in it together. It's not Mum and Dad bossing everyone. It's their life, their goals, their responsibility, our family support system, and our choice to help others. Giving them time to do this develops planning, written and oral communication, and family connectedness.

If your children are younger than my age group (12-18), you can simplify it. One goal (pick up toys), with more regular and smaller rewards (weekly) will work just as well. The principle is for everyone to feel that the family is theirs to look after, to contribute to, and to do their best for. Ownership builds connection, which builds communication.

Written Language

Reading is another way we can show our children how to love words and language, and in many ways it pre-empts writing. Reading to children under five, and even when they can read themselves, has been proven again and again to have benefits for their future (Merga, 2017). When we read to our child and sit close by them it continues to develop physical and emotional security, and this physical connectedness increases attachment. They also begin to recognise the shapes and sounds of letters and words, and this firms up the sounds and meanings within their mind. Children begin to understand sentence structure, tone of voice, and hidden meanings (inference and sarcasm) through hearing language spoken and relating it to text.

If we remember that children's brains are like sponges and that they absorb everything they experience, we can understand why they get stuck on a particular book time and time again. If you have ever read to young children, you will know what I mean. I own a much worn out, dog eared copy of The Cat in the Hat by Dr Seuss. In fact, I have read that book so many times to eager children that I can recite it word for word!

While this can get irritating for us as adults, for children it is heaven. They find much joy and pleasure in the simple flow and rhythm of the words. In the consistency and in predicting

The close attachment along with the words of the story provides a space for your child to develop their own language abilities.

what will come next. When young children read or are read to, they begin to love the experience, and it is that love of learning that will see them becoming lifelong learners.

Reading and writing also encourages children to focus. We have an epidemic of unfocused and distracted children in schools. When we read to children and take the time to encourage and help them with their learning, they see that we value what they do, and they will try even harder to do well. Children love to please adults. Your child loves to please you. At their most basic level they all want our love and affirmation. If we sit with them and write together, showing them how to do it, reading to them and listening to them read to us, it develops the ability to recall what is being said and eventually apply it to other parts of their lives. It increases intelligence, it motivates them to do their best, and it is the best way to encourage them to learn.

The more they experience, the more they can recall and the more that they can use this knowledge in their lives. Because at the end of the day, knowledge without application is useless. We can bridge that gap by discussing the reading and writing that they are learning.

'Reading and writing also encourages children to focus. We have an epidemic of unfocused and distracted children in schools'.

John Hattie (2018), an educational researcher, has found that the single most important practice in education is collective teacher efficacy. This means that when a child does something that is incorrect, the best thing to do is to clearly explain why it is incorrect and how to do it correctly. The feedback is specific and is best if it is put into practice straight away, such as repeating a math question with the right workflow or spelling a word the correct way.

This principle can also apply to parents at home. If you want your child to do the best they can in school, then work with them. Check their work and explain the correct answer if they need it. This is best done in an encouraging, uplifting way, rather than demanding and heavy-handed.

With young children we read with them, and capture their thoughts by writing for them. This releases their intellectual potential and models for them the writing process. One of the best things we can do for our children is to help them become curious about the world around them and instill in them a love of learning. Of course, books are not the only way to learn, but they are a great way to introduce self-directed learning and improve written communication, which will all help children succeed to their fullest potential.

Success in this case is the ability to understand other peoples' thoughts and opinions through the written word. Reading with and to children can give them this love and enjoyment of learning. Using the relationship we have built with them to engage them in the written word is a win-win for all. It gives the children the pure enjoyment of being lost in a story from someone else's imagination as well as a safe place to explore this concept. Imagine living each day with a passion and desire to find out what the day holds and all that can be discovered! That sounds like a recipe for adventure and a satisfying life to me – and one that children can find in books.

Once our children have this love of reading, it can then be expanded into writing, so that our children can share their imaginations with others. Their vocabulary, understanding of sentence structure and syntax will develop exponentially with increased reading.

Speaking Two Languages

Research has shown learning multiple languages in childhood increases both the grey and white matter in the brain, and that these changes continue throughout life if the languages are both used consistently (Pliatsikas, 2015). If this sounds like a different language to you, let me just make it clear that this is a good thing! More bumpy bits in the brain, the more matter, the more neural connections, the more ways we can use them, the more intelligence.

It is said that children learn a new language easiest under the age of seven years old. At this time the brain is growing at its fastest, which means connections can be made quicker and the child has more complex brain activity in the language centres at a younger age. This isn't to say that monolingual children are less intelligent, it just demonstrates that we can help our children's brain formation and growth through the environment we raise them in. The more we input, the more they can output, so to speak. So, if you have the opportunity, don't be afraid to teach your child multiple languages and consistently use them. And if English isn't your first language that doesn't mean your child will be disadvantaged. They can pick any language up easily enough with the right consistency. We can never talk too much to our children; therefore keep on talking, explaining, pronouncing and lovingly guiding them. And when they can't stop talking back to us, well, that's when we just pray for patience!

We have seen that by talking and communicating we show love. When we love someone deeply words will often flow from us no matter what language we speak. We really don't need to think about them, and it often doesn't even matter what we are saying. When we use positive words of love and encouraging tones of voice it can change who our children are, what they think of themselves, and what they do in life. These words are far better for our children's language development and self-esteem than simply instructional communication. Instructional words sound like 'do this', 'come here', 'do that', and very easily become automatic. Sometimes as busy parents it is easy to fall into that trap. I will put my hand up for that.

Instructional words tell the child what to do, and some of this is necessary of course, but when we use expressive communication it adds emotion, thought and creativity to a child. It teaches them to see themselves as in control of their language and gives them the permission to share their thoughts and feelings as a valid person - no matter their age.

Practical Steps for Language Development

- Read to your child

- Listen to them read to you

- Help them write a story

- Help them work through homework

- Teach them a new language

- Ask for their thoughts and opinions

- Use positive words

- Gently correct them if they use the wrong word or grammar

By now I am sure you see that words have a powerful impact FOR our children. But what about the impact they have IN our children? Are all things equal when it comes to language? Well the reality is—not really.

Gottman (2017), has undertaken research showing that for marriages to work there needs to be a 5:1 ratio of positive to negative words. Kvols (1998) states that children hear 432 negative words for every 32 positive words. That feels extreme doesn't it? But before you go down 'parenting guilt lane' let's unpack this more.

What are your thoughts about the language you use with your children? If your goal is change, I encourage you to be honest with yourself.

Note one or two words you would like to remove from your communication with your children, and what you will replace them with.

My earlier story of my negative words to my son is just one example of many times where I have been too tired, too busy and too angry to make the right choice with my words. We are human and it happens to all of us. Getting things wrong is a part of life, don't accept guilt. We are busy, multitasking parents and when we have a few little mites running around our feet all day draining every ounce of our energy, it can be super hard to say, 'please sweetie come and play inside rather than on the road'! Slightly tongue in cheek, but it's true isn't it?

Sometimes we can barely say nice things in our own heads let alone out of our mouths to children who are drawing all over the car, round and round with a permanent marker! (Yes, that's another true story!)

But we really do speak life or death over our children with our words. We either build them up or tear them down. Think of it from their perspective. To these little people we are the most important thing in their lives, and if we are angry and mean with our words, what will they think of themselves? That they are bad and naughty.

Just as we feel that pang of guilt, we can take a breath and know that we have another chance to try again. Let go of the guilt and start again, right now. Commit to making small changes every day. Try to speak more positively to your children, knowing that as you set the example for them, they will follow in your footsteps and do as you do.

You can do it! Just start small; one change and you and your child will feel much better for it. Often, we need to consciously fill ourselves with positivity so that we can share that with our children. This is a lifelong learning curve, one step at a time.

One word at a time. I tell my kids, 'If you do right, you'll feel right. Do good, you'll feel good'. Do or say one thing that you know you should, even if you don't feel like it, and it will make you feel like the best parent in the world.

'A simple thing like changing an instruction can have a huge impact on changing your child's behaviour if it is carried out consistently over time'.

TEACHER'S CORNER

As teachers, many of us are familiar with the research into how the brain responds to words that are said. For example, if I say 'don't think of a giant green monkey' what do you automatically think of? A giant green monkey, don't you? To the brain it doesn't make any difference if we say do or don't. The words are heard and that is what the brain thinks about. We need to remember to tell children about the action that we WANT rather than what we don't want. Here are some examples.

Words to say	Rather than
I need you to pick up those toys on the floor.	Stop tipping out those toys.
It's inside time in 2 minutes.	Why are you still outside?
Use gentle hands with your friends.	Stop hitting your friends.
It's time to sit quietly now.	Stop your talking!
Did you have an accident?	Why did you make such a mess?

The emphasis is always on the action that we want the child to do rather than drawing their attention to what we don't want them to do. It is framing the words positively rather than negatively. A simple thing like changing an instruction can have a huge impact on changing your child's behaviour if it is carried out consistently over time.

Ideas for Change

As parents we are responsible to model good language and encourage it through positive words. We determine the course of our own lives and the course of our children's lives by our words. Imagine being told 'you're dumb' for your whole life. How do you think the child will grow up to feel? Intelligent? No—dumb, absolutely. Even, if it is said 'jokingly' all the time.

Remember, children don't know themselves; they find themselves through the words and actions of others. We have immense potential to shape our child's future with positive words and experiences. And when we get it wrong, seek forgiveness from them, forgive yourself and move on.

Most of this chapter has focused on children's language under five years old. This is because of the brain growth and the window of opportunity we have to make meaningful deposits into our children's development. However, the importance of language does not stop there. By extending vocabulary at age appropriate times our children build on these solid foundations and increase their capacity for more complex skills. They may not grow up to be English professors, but having skills in the language they speak not only ensures strong brain pathways in the language centre, it also allows them to contribute positively throughout their life.

What are you going to commit to change? Write it below in a positively framed sentence and repeat it to yourself a few times. Practice on yourself what you intend to do for your children.

DAD'S SAY

I am Samoan/Fijian and I was brought up speaking both languages by both sides of my family. On my Fijian side I learnt the language mostly in church, and I learnt Samoan through everyday life experience at home. I remember being around my aunties and uncles in my younger years, who naturally spoke their language, and we either responded in Samoan or English. One of the main reasons my parents moved to New Zealand was so we could have a better life and more opportunities.

Taking my kids around to their grandparents, who speak to them in Samoan or Fijian, is a good thing for so many reasons. Simple day-to-day language such as 'close the door', or 'make a tea please', or 'how is school?' can teach them a lot. I can see my kids understand the tone, the look on my mum's face, putting all of it together, working out what's being said and formulating a reply. There's a lot more to it than 'just learning another language'. It's finding the best way that is most authentic.

For me as a young fella I remember my dad helping me with basic homework such as reading, writing and math. However, it wasn't very consistent, and the teaching styles back then were very old school. My schooling reflected this as a kid. I didn't do well and didn't learn to enjoy it.

Now as an adult I have studied for a bachelor's degree, and my job involves a lot of reading and writing, but outside of that, I wouldn't volunteer to do more. I believe if reading and writing were consistently encouraged in my earlier years it would have made me feel different about education as an adult. This has also influenced how I relate to my own children. I understand that consistency is essential.

As a dad, one of the main things that has helped me teach my children has been to apply the things I have learnt about love languages and then see how it impacts my relationships with them. It sounds easy to do, but it's hard when you have a large family. Over the years I quickly learnt that the love languages were more than just knowing each of my kids' individual love language, they were also key to understanding how to discipline, or make decisions with their language in mind. That in the end they still feel loved and supported by their dad.

For example, I have learnt that shouting at my second eldest boy will not work for him. I am human. I get angry and I have yelled. But for him it just shuts him down. Even if I am explaining a task that he has been told many times to do or telling him off about something he has done wrong — yelling doesn't work. The reason being is that one of his top love languages is words of affirmation.

In the past I used to physically discipline my children and my parenting style was 'My way or the highway'. I remember yelling at him to make sure he got the message loud and clear. That message was 'Do what you are told!' I am not proud of this, and there have been many things I have had to learn to become a better father. Part of this for me was to learn to deal with my anger, and deal with the past. This was important for me to do and the love languages helped to change this and become a main driving force of my parenting.

Discovering my own love language helped with this process. I slowly learnt that responding in the way of the child's love language has more power than my hands or voice. I have learnt and tried different ways—even ways that initially felt weird to me, such as cuddles (even though he is 6 ft. 2") and sending texts to him at school. I can see these things mean a lot to him. I'm still on the journey of being Super Dad, but I'm far away from the dad that I was. Understanding their love languages, and how to communicate with these through their different ages has helped me have a better relationship with them.

Language Through the Middle Years

Practical ways you can encourage your child to read through the middle years is to offer a range of books, both fiction and non-fiction, newspaper articles, and blogs—to expand their general knowledge and allow them to gain eloquence in the written word. Talking about these things will also increase their verbal language skills, and a good debate will help them to articulate why they should stick up for their viewpoint.

My daughter has learnt that the best way to get what she is asking for is to present to me the benefits of what she wants and how it will help us all. She has learnt to negotiate pocket money, bedtimes, and privileges this way. She convinces me that what she wants will help everyone, and that inspires me to see things from her point of view. Much better than whining and moaning which gets an immediate 'no' from me. She is currently trying to convince me that she needs a cell phone. Our current rule stands that the kids get one when they are 14; she is nearly 13. She has negotiated that she is more mature, more responsible, and needs it more than her brothers did at that age. She has some valid arguments and her ability to reason and communicate her needs shows me that she has put time and effort into her thoughts. She still hasn't got the phone, but she is determined to show me through words and action that she is responsible enough for it.

Without trying to sound too 1950's, the dinner table is a fantastic place to discuss world, life, or school issues—it gives children a way to process their day. As the older children share the new things they have learnt, the younger children then start to pick up on the language and become familiar with mature concepts (Harbec, 2017). It becomes an enjoyable time for everyone. No growling or instructing, it's completely non-threatening. Just having a discussion, as you would with adults. The children tend to relax more at this time, when there is food, and fun and laughter. It creates a sense of ease where they are more open to communicate. Some of the best memories can be created as you sit around a dinner table discussing life.

Recently, during family time together, my 12-year-old was telling us that they were learning about force and energy at school. Suddenly a spontaneous game emerged where we would question the energy that different items in the house had and estimate the force it would take to move each one. It was quite hilarious to hear some of the guesses, and then the responses from the more logical thinkers.

At this time our 10-year-old thought he was amazing if he could answer first—even if he got it completely wrong. We could see their personalities coming out, and how they solved problems. I didn't initiate this or sit down and plan what to discuss at dinner time. It took no extra effort than just getting dinner on the table and asking them what they learnt about that day. We have covered a range of topics this way, from racism to earthquakes and natural disasters, to where babies come from, just to name a few.

The extension of language for our middle-aged children happens when we are talking naturally with them, helping them with homework and just being presently involved in their lives. Every now and then there will be a word you can correct pronunciation on, or a sentence that needs to be restructured. There are new words to learn, and tones of voice to communicate different meanings. These learnings happen more naturally in the middle years and provide us a way to build deeper relationships with our children.

The middle years are a beautiful time where children still want to be with you and want to do things together. Utilize this inner drive. Do something they want to do together and then just talk. Maybe it's fixing the bike, or building a ramp, or looking in shops. This time together will lead naturally into discussions and communication.

'...the dinner table is a fantastic place to discuss world, life, or school issues—it gives them a way to process their day'.

Language Through the Teen Years

I am still in the midst of the whirlwind that is the teenage years. Storms have brewed, come and gone, and I am sure there will be others headed my way. I do not consider myself an expert in this area, but I know there are some lessons I have learnt the hard way. I have learnt that one of my biggest roles in their teen years is to take the time and create the space for them to talk. The release of their pent-up emotions will help them solve their own problems many times. When they are exhibiting behaviour I may not approve of it is often because they feel that no one is listening to and understanding them. They feel they can't talk to anyone so they think on their own, make wrong decisions and feel horrible about it. This creates a cycle where they are more prone to give up and give in than push through what it is they are struggling with. They need to know that someone is on their side. The old analogy of a coach is true. Someone to cheer them on, guide them, and support them through their choices, and consequences of their choices.

In all honesty, being a sounding board isn't my strength. By nature, I am a problem solver, and I really struggle to sit and just listen and listen and listen to the same stuff over and over again. I want to get in there and help solve it, make everyone happy, and move on. But it just doesn't work like this in the teen world. They have crazy hormones and often only half a brain! There is so much change physiologically through the teen years that impacts every area of their being – emotional, spiritual, physical, social and cognitive. They are becoming their own person and need to make their own decisions. They want the time and space to trust themselves to solve their own problems and to grow in independence. Yet they also want the close relationship of a true supporter.

This is why one of the biggest things we can do to develop language in our teens is to help them have the words and emotional resilience to express themselves respectfully. Of course, we do this through modelling (showing them how by doing it ourselves), but we also do it by giving words to their emotions when they can't find any. It is important to encourage them to speak (or write) when they can't put words to feelings, and to teach them how to take responsibility for the words that they use.

For us, we have firm rules around the language used in our house. I do not allow my children to use profanity. They are teens, so I'm sure they have done so, just as those words have on occasion been heard flying around our house (we are not perfect either!). But all my children understand that it is not an acceptable use of language. That is not what we use everyday. I do not overlook it. I do not write it off as teen behaviour, and I do not laugh at it. I correct it or simply let them know that it isn't acceptable in our house. I believe that the use of that kind of language shows a lack of imagination and vocabulary. I give them alternative words, words of respect. I demonstrate sophisticated language because often in society we are judged by the language we use. (Whether this is right or wrong is for another debate). 'Just because everyone else is doing it' is not a good enough reason for my family to do it. I ensure that they understand that they are in part defined by their language, and in part their language defines them and profanity serves them no positive purpose. This is again the power of words.

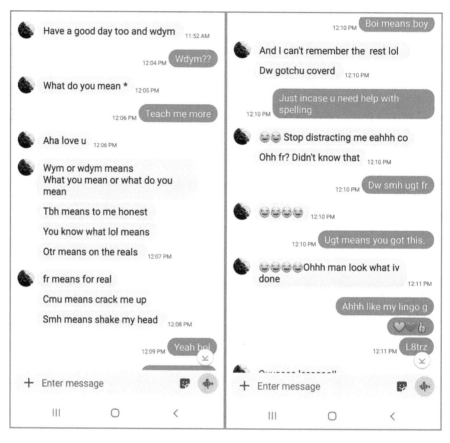

Here is a text conversation between my teen and I. I am in dark green, his replies in grey. Sometimes we just gotta have a bit of fun with it all!

It is harder at this age because we are relinquishing control over our children. They are becoming adults, and they need to make their own choices. There needs to be some form of freedom, though I do believe that while the children live in our house, it is the adults who need to establish and enforce these boundaries. This shouldn't be a hard and heavy thing. It is just how it is. A common agreement to abide by the rules so that the family can function in peace. Just like a mini society. And teenagers are more willing to jump on board with this if you are also following the same rules. They can smell hypocrisy a mile away and that just won't work with them.

I also teach my children to greet people respectfully. To shake hands, look people in the eye, and use appropriate and kind language— because other people matter as well. They are taught that from a young age and I feel it is just as important when they are teens to uphold that standard.

Sometimes it is hard just to get time to talk to your teens. I encourage you to turn off the devices and spend time trying to engage with them and talk about what they are thinking about. See if you can build on your relationship with them by understanding life from their point of view. Even if the TV is off just through dinner time it will still provide an opportunity which wasn't there before. It may be awkward at first, and you may even have to find the dinner table! However, in time, I am sure you will see that it can be a relaxed, comfortable and fun routine. It feels really good to be connected to your children. But it won't happen by chance, it really won't. You will need to be intentional about setting boundaries around the devices and rules around meal times. You can start small, just once a week. Let them know what is happening and be prepared for some whinging and moaning until they experience how cool it is. Persevere, my friend.

Action Points

What was your biggest 'ah-ha!' moment of this section?

What change are you immediately going to make?

Imagine what the world would be like if we all did this together. If we were purposeful about a journey of attachment, filled with language, reading, connection and love. We might just have a **Natural Childhood Movement.**

Top Three Points to Ponder

- You are your child's first teacher, never outsource this responsibility to schools, professionals or devices – you matter more than you realise. Your participation is vital.

- Create a love of learning in your child by modelling, encouraging, and introducing them to multiple forms of language as much as possible throughout all their years.

- The more we put into our children in the early years, the more they can draw from in their later years. The first years of a child's life are crucial—but it's never too late to start – talk, talk, talk.

'Encouraging a child means that one or more of the following critical life messages are coming through, either by word or by action: I believe in you, I trust you, I know you can handle this, you are listened to, you are cared for, you are very important to me'.

~ **Barbara Coloroso**

L·O·V·E
Outdoors

Outdoors

Outdoors, n. Any area outside buildings or shelter, typically far away from human habitation.

> The **outdoors** nurtures a love and appreciation of nature, our connection to the land, the stewardship and ecosystem link, and living sustainably. It is space to breathe, and think, and rest, and be at peace. It is our connection to our roots and a reminder of our place in this world. It is simplicity, wholeness, curiosity.

I love summer. I really, really, love summer. One reason why I love it so much is because I see my children free. Some of my best childhood memories were of long, hot days at the beach. We arrived as a family early in the morning in our togs and we barely saw our parents all day. We would pick pipis (shellfish) first, digging into the sand with our toes to find them through squelching sand, and then scoop all the wet soggy-ness out until our fingernails were full of it. We would collect a bucket or two and even crack some open to eat raw while we continued our hunt. We would return the buckets and just as quickly run straight back out to the water. We would splash and slide through the warm water with the sun beating down on us. Sand covering our entire bodies and caking our hair into a matted mess. We would carry on in that way until our stomachs rumbled with hunger and our skin pricked with the burn. These days would end dirty, tired, sunburnt and sore, but satisfied. Oh, so satisfied. We would sleep like babies. Those nights we felt as free and contented as birds.

I decided before I ever had my children that they would be free to explore and enjoy the outdoors. It would be their time to be away from jobs and responsibilities, it would be their space.

As humans we are made to connect with the outdoors. No matter what belief system we align ourselves with or aspire to, it all is closely connected to the outdoors, to nature, to Earth. Evolution acknowledges primate mammals as part of our history, being a part of the natural primal earth. Christianity acknowledges that we are formed from the dust of the earth. Hindus acknowledge the co-dependence of all life upon each other and Buddhists seek to live in peace and harmony with all of nature, being all is one. New Age beliefs are based on our connection to the energy released by the electromagnetic fields of our world. From traditional legends and myths of old, to more modern new-age thought there is an understanding that we as a human race are closely linked and tied to the earth that we live in. It is in this space that we can agree that we as people groups have strong and spiritual connections to nature. There is something beyond us that ties us to our earth, and if we pause for a moment, we can physically feel that connection.

The Impact on our Body

Throughout history humans have relied upon and been intricately connected to the outdoors, nature and the physical environment. There really is no argument that we should not remain connected. The progression of human life throughout time, irrespective of race and culture, has needed a close connection with the outdoors to sustain life. Food, water, shelter, community, and progression of our species have all relied on our physical world. It is only in recent history that we have drastically moved away from symbiosis with the world to the misuse of the natural materials it gives us.

This separation from the natural world has had a huge impact on our own species as well as all other living creatures. We have never been as sick, over-diagnosed, medicated and stressed as we are now. It is currently common for Doctors and therapists to be in high demand because of the toll our modern way of living is taking on our physical bodies. Constant sitting, watching screens, convenience foods and a convenient lifestyle is damaging our species like nothing ever seen before. And all of the above, which aren't bad things in themselves, accumulate to separate us more and more from our connection to the earth and build dependence on ease.

For example, would it be an accurate guess that your children watch TV for an hour a day? I would guess that in most households that is a conservative figure. But let's say just one hour. Over a week that's seven hours of sitting and screens. Seven hours in itself, may not be too damaging for children. But let's also assume, your children are dropped off to and picked up from school—quite common for modern day busy living. That is approximately 2 hours in the car. Then there will be the travel to after-school activities, there will be movie nights, cell phone use, and appointments...you get the picture.

There are the many additional hours that children spend in front of computers for school work, then they come home and spend up to three hours on computers for homework! How many hours are we up to now with sitting and screen time? I have lost count. But the point is clear. This is modern life. This is expected. The schools are not pushing a physical curriculum anymore either. It's STEM (Science, Technology, Engineering, Maths), and STEAM (Science, Technology, Engineering, Arts, Maths), if you are lucky. Our children are sitting longer, watching more, being entertained rather than creative, being busy rather than productive, and we as parents are living the same lives as well. We aren't getting outside as much as we need or even want to. Therefore, we need to take purposeful action to make a change.

So, what is the answer for our children? How do we raise the next generation to be a more well-rounded holistic balanced society? How can we create a balance where we use all the benefits of modern technology to our advantage, but still maintain our connection to our Earth? Challenging questions, but there are answers out there.

It will take mindful action to change the future of our children. Each and every decision we make has a ripple effect. Each action we reinforce creates habits and patterns of living. It is simple to say and challenging to do, but we must make the time to enjoy the outdoors and eagerly connect our children to it at all costs. If we determine to take small steps towards what we believe is important eventually those steps will be leaps and bounds.

Have a think about your routine. How many hours do you think your children spend on devices? Or sitting inside?

How many hours have they been outside connected to the natural world?

In some ways the change from an indoor to intentionally outdoor life is really just a small step. Generally, most cities are equipped with many different and cost-free parks, playgrounds and outdoor areas. We do not need to go far before we can access stimulating outdoor environments for our children. As much as you can let your children explore and test their boundaries in the outdoors. You may also find that you enjoy and benefit from it just as much as they do.

The Body's Fuel

As we explore and become refreshed and excited about the outdoors, a natural next step might be to consider the way we are eating and what food we are giving our children. This can be a difficult topic for many parents and a source of the dreaded 'parent guilt'—I have been there, so I completely understand if that is where you are right now. But I have learnt some guiding principles that have helped me, no matter whether I was broke or if I had money, which I will discuss later.

The actual physical formation of the brain is defined by what we eat. This is incredible. What we put into our mouths as young children either helps or hinders our brain's development. For this reason, a lack of proper nutrition can have lasting physical impact on the size, shape and functioning of the brain (Melillo, 2016). Food is literally the fuel the body uses to grow and develop, inside and out.

We don't have to look far before we see the impact of malnutrition on children's development, including thinking and learning. This is not just a lack of quantity of food, but a lack of food that nourishes the body with the right minerals, vitamins, fats and energy. Our food really does make us.

This can be easier said than done though can't it? We all have a pretty good idea of what and when and how we should be eating but it's often hard to do it. There are practical barriers such as cost, time and the availability of food, and there are social barriers such as a fast food culture and peer pressures. Then there are psychological barriers for example, how we think about food and what it means to us emotionally. All of these things are before we even come to the physical needs of hunger; what we really need versus what we want.

Food doesn't just feed our bodies and fuel us, it gives us pleasure, feelings of connection and memories of emotion. Who doesn't have a food memory from childhood? It is for this reason that our culture plays a huge part in how, when and what we eat. And every culture has specific ways they enjoy food and their own beliefs about food. We can enjoy our cultures, whatever they are, celebrate all their strengths, and at the same time reflect on our beliefs and learn which foods can best serve us.

For me, as a New Zealand European, bread has been a staple of our family. Sandwiches in the lunchbox, homemade bread rolls after school (delish with melted butter and marmite!), soup with bread, wraps and filled rolls, and toast for breakfast. I love bread, but the older I get the more I realise bread doesn't serve me well, and not all breads are equally nutritious. There is an influx of research and information about how our bodies process it (or don't process it) and the impact it has on us. Do

I still eat it – yes. Do my children – yes. The details of nutrition are not my area of expertise, but with all the information we have out there we can be informed about how the foods we are eating are impacting our children's health, concentration and learning.

I'm not saying that bread is the big baddie, it is just one example from my experience. But it goes to show that the tide of opinion can change on foods we once considered healthy. We need to examine our beliefs about health and food regularly in the light of new science, so that we can maximise our wellbeing. We have an amazing opportunity to provide our children with the best fuel for their bodies, and fast track their health, energy and brain growth, as well as reducing illness. I encourage you to be open to new ideas around your family's food. To examine your personal beliefs about what is healthy or not, and see if there are some small changes you can make in your life.

I personally don't prescribe to a specific diet and this section is not about telling you what to let your children eat or not eat. I have tried many different things myself. I have learnt and am still learning what works for us and what doesn't. This is my encouragement to you. Do some reading on the subject. Listen to the experts. Be open to change and curious about what you don't know. Knowledge changes and grows through time, the thoughts around healthy food in the 90's were quite different to what is accepted today. If we change our beliefs, our actions change with them, and this will ultimately help our children become all they can be.

'Food doesn't just feed our bodies and fuel us, it gives us pleasure, feelings of connection and memories of emotion. Who doesn't have a food memory from childhood?'

I also believe we can't really go too wrong if we stick to natural things. If we eat what the earth produces, and don't mess around too much with it, then it will be best for us. Unfortunately, it is very hard these days to know which of our foods has been modified, or how many nutrients they contain, but natural fruit and vegetables and ethical meat is a fair place to start. I would love to buy local organic food all the time, however this isn't always possible as I am often feeding 7+ people per night (including ravenous teen boys who can out-eat their 6 ft 4" father!). I do make the effort to eat this way as often as I am able even if that is not as much as I would like. But I am on the journey, which is where I encourage you to be too. It has certainly become a lot easier to recognize processed foods these days, and the more we can stay away from these, the better for us all. If something comes pre-packaged, made in a factory, filled with words you don't understand – then that is probably not something you need to be consuming.

I don't prescribe whole heartedly to one specific regime and I don't like overly restrictive diets, but if many experts in the field are making the same recommendations then I think it is worthwhile to take note of it and try it for yourself. The key is to remember that what matters most is what we do every day rather than what we do now and then. If takeaways and processed foods is a 'now and then' occurrence for you then you are on the right track to improving your health. Check out the further reading section in the back if you are keen to learn more about this topic.

Money and affordability always play into the food we eat. It can be very expensive to eat 'healthy' and that can be a barrier to providing wholesome nutrition for our children. Also, 'healthy' isn't always as healthy as it is claimed to be and can be just trumped-up marketing. If we focus on the right size portions for our growing children, whole fruits, vegetables and grains, as well as natural sources of protein, I think they will be okay! If you can't afford quinoa at $49.00kg or pine nuts at $99.00kg, don't worry! Just leave them out. We don't have to eat them just because someone says they are 'healthy' or a 'superfood'. There are still plenty of other, more affordable healthy foods out there.

A food preparation concept that has been around for generations but is now becoming more and more popular is fermentation. This is an age-old way of ensuring food lasts a long time and maximises the nutrients by generating probiotics. If you aren't familiar with fermentation, think kombucha, kefir, sauerkraut, kimchi, some soya sauces and fish sauces. It is using natural good bacteria to add probiotics to your food. These probiotics are so important for our gut health. There are millions of bacteria inside our intestines. When we are sick, this often means that the bad bacteria have outnumbered the good. However, by eating naturally fermented foods, we can introduce and increase the amount of good bacteria in our stomachs. Fermented food has been linked to overall better health, better brain function, and more energy and focus. Isn't that something we want for our children?

Often, we need to trust our instincts and go back to how Grandma used to cook. The simple recipes we remember from our childhood are often some of the cheapest and healthiest methods of cooking. The latest cooking shows and fads are great to watch, but they are not always practical, affordable or healthy! Sometimes just a small adjustment makes a huge difference, such as planning in advance, cooking from scratch and changing our value systems to prioritise health as well as understanding a bit more about nutrition. Plus there is huge satisfaction in knowing that you have made something that both nourishes and satisfies your family!

A Trip Down Memory Lane

As a 20-year-old wife and mother, cooking was a shock to my system. I was brought up on good food but I never really had an interest in making it. I had been vegetarian for 10 years, and had just married a carnivore! Add a wee baby, all the should and should nots of feeding him, coupled with a grocery budget of $60 a week (including nappies, etc.) - I was overwhelmed. Cooking wasn't a choice for me, it was a necessity. It wasn't to be trendy or delicious, it was just plain need.

For those first years my cooking philosophy was literally 'How can I get the healthiest, most filling food for the lowest cost'. It has been because of this need that I read and practiced, learned and cooked, frozen and pickled, sauced and... well it goes on and on. I had to feed my family. I value health. How could I do both?

Home cooking is making a real comeback now, nearly twenty years later. We are seeing that the old-fashioned way of eating was good for us and the planet. Using the whole animal, the whole plant; and whatever is in season is best for us, our children and the planet. Cooking up a roast or a stew using the juices from the meat is not only sustainable, it's good for you too (according to a paleo/ketogenic diet). Growing vegetables and using the whole plant is sustainable, cost effective and healthy. Using food that is in season saves you money—especially if someone has a garden and is giving it to you free.

Over the last few years, as my mum has been getting older, we have 'cook up' days, something that I rope my kids into helping with. I even have friends joining in to bottle, pickle, and ferment together. Learning together and getting the satisfaction that what we have put on the table is of true value to our families is very fulfilling. We know the ingredients, we can reduce or omit sugar, and we provide food for months ahead. No unnatural preservatives, additives, colours, or E numbers. Natural, whole, healthy food, and all it takes is some time and a willingness to learn. A full day in the kitchen can give you pickles and sauces for the year. Sometimes the children don't like it, but other times I'm surprised how much they do. It has become one of my creative outlets. Learning about food and health and then seeing what I have, or what is in season and creating things according to our tastes. Just experiment a little - put things together and see how they work.

Ideas for Change

If you are keen on trying this kind of natural experimentation with food and you don't know where to start, don't stress. This is definitely not a prerequisite to being a great mum, but if you are wanting to give it a go here are some guidelines:

1) Talk a kid or two into helping you – or a good friend who is keen to learn

2) Find something cheap or free to experiment with (e.g., cucumbers are 3 for $3 or cheaper in the peak season).

3) Search for a recipe that is in line with how you want to eat (e.g., health values such as sugar free, gluten free, fermentation etc.).

4) Now go for it! Even if it goes wrong, there are usually a few other things you can turn it into to save it. Just Google ideas (e.g. if your bottled peaches didn't work,

then just stew them up and have them on your cereal for breakfast, or put them in muffins etc.).

5) Remember it is all about the process not just the product. Enjoy your time with your children and the freedom to be creative.

As I write this, I have two full loquat trees in the backyard ready to harvest. I am now searching for recipes to use. I will bottle these so we don't waste them and can have them year round. It is all about experimenting a little; however, I might draw the line at making loquat liqueur!

I totally understand that it can feel overwhelming when we start to look at what we 'should' do to feed our kids healthily. We are told that vegan is the way, or paleo, or low fat, or low sugar or low carb, and then there are a list of allergies that they might suffer from. We were told that balance of food is important and not to limit food groups, and now we are told that the food pyramid we were taught as children should be turned upside down! It's definitely confusing and difficult to get a clear message on what we should do. So I read. I read a lot. I know my kids and my husband, and I know what they like and how much they eat. I try to take a little bit of everything and make small changes to our habits to make it work for us. A smaller portion. Brown rice instead of white. Less carbohydrates. No sugar or sugar alternatives. A healthier way of cooking the meals they love. It can give you quite a buzz to know that the food you are dishing up—even on a strict budget—is healthy and nutritious and nourishes your family. There is real satisfaction in that.

I feel passionate about healthy choices because of the increase in child obesity. The number of children diagnosed is increasing drastically and is almost becoming acceptable in society. This really breaks my heart because we are setting our children up for long-term and sometimes lifelong health issues. We are forming the habits that will destroy them. We love our children so much and food is often a way of showing love. But let's not harm them with this love. Sometimes it is simply education and willpower that is needed to change the course of our children's lives. Experts recognise the importance of habits in the early years of a child's life as they help determine actions in their future. We can set our children up for success by teaching them and discussing how to choose healthier foods.

The food we eat has huge significance on our children's development. It really is an area of LOVE we cannot overlook if we want to set them up for success. Do your best and keep trying to do better. Don't accept any guilt. Acknowledge where you are and just take one step further.

This week I am going to commit to:

Long term I would like to see my family (eating, doing, and living):

I will get support from:

Impact on our Brain

It is not only to avoid negative consequences that we should spend time outside, but it is also to gain all the positive benefits. Science is now proving just how much our bodies need to be outdoors. There are studies showing that by being outside daily we are more likely to live longer, enjoy better health and maintain strong brain function throughout our entire lives! And who doesn't want that for themselves and their children? Professor John Ratey, in his book Spark (2010), shows through case studies, research and experience that maintaining a connection with the outdoors leaves lasting physical benefits for us, e.g., reduced risk of diseases, cancer, and stress (just to name a few). These benefits work just as well in adults as they do children. It is never too late to start to set your whole family up for success.

In another of Ratey's books, Go Wild (2014), he maintains that running barefoot through unstable terrain increases brain functioning and development and can potentially add years to your life. It is like a natural high for the brain, where your brain is put on high alert and forms new neural connections because of it. This, coupled with healthy eating of whole, natural foods, provides the body the energy it needs for optimal function. This is the best environment for our brains to develop and function, no matter our age. The principle of the outdoors is about going back to nature and doing what we are designed to do. Eat from the land, move around on the land, and do this in the context of secure relationships.

I am not saying that our children need to turn into Tarzan or need to be cavemen to ensure they are gaining all the benefits from a natural childhood outdoors (though many of them would probably love the opportunity to try). However, by living by the outdoors principle we are creating wonder in our children, and a curiosity about the world around them. This is intrinsic to young children.

'The principle of the outdoors is about going back to nature and doing what we are designed to do. Eat from the land, move around on the land, and do this in the context of secure relationships.'

The outdoors encourages our children to be investigators and explorers and to connect to something that is deeper and bigger than themselves. We are acknowledging hundreds of years of human evolution and paying tribute to the land that has sustained us for so long. And while we are doing all of this we are living our best lives and supporting long, satisfying life. We are making our bodies stronger and increasing the neural pathways in our brain. We are enhancing our sensory perception and inviting a sense of peace. We are understanding our place and role on this earth.

As humans we have such a huge impact on this earth. The smallness of our frame, yet the largeness of our responsibility. When we are in the outdoors, our children are understanding our place in a much larger ecosystem, where every aspect is connected and networked together. Who knew that being outside could offer us all of this? As well as being the answer to many of our problems? Are you ready to set foot out your back door yet?

Have you ever smelled the fresh clean scent of recently mowed grass on a spring morning, or felt the warm sunshine on your back while your ears pick up the gentle crashing of waves? Maybe you have experienced the powerful crash of thunder overhead, with heavy rain and hard hail pelting on a tin roof, or the wild frenzy of wind whipping up sand around your legs, stinging your skin like needles?

As you read these words, your brain imagines these things happening and your body feels these sensations. This is the power of experience. This is the power of physically being in a new place experiencing new things. These experiences never leave us, they become us and become the context from which future learning stems.

'Are you ready to set foot out your back door yet?'

A Trip Down Memory Lane

I remember as a child my family lived in a small town of a couple of thousand. We were only twenty minutes away from the city, but that was enough to separate us from the hustle and bustle of city living. Though money wasn't free flowing in our home we still had the best experiences with the outdoors.

Our playgrounds were the local mountain, the forest and the town lake which was built from an abandoned quarry. As we grew older, we were allowed to pack food and go off up the mountain for half a day or so. We needed to fend off cows, navigate jolting electric fences, and push through the physical exhaustion just to reach the top. We would picnic there, with stunning 360 degree views as our backdrop, breathing in the freshness of the air and feeling the warm grass beneath us. These moments with friends, exploring our area and creating our own imaginary world gave freedom, independence, risk and reward.

Sometimes I would go bareback riding on my friend's horses through the forest. With nothing but a horse and reins. The musky smell of the earthy trees filled our noses while the clopping of the hooves thudded on hard ground. The ache in your legs from gripping on for dear life to a horse's back brought satisfaction and a feeling of being able to accomplish anything. These treasured memories of my childhood were spent alone, without adult supervision, even without a cellphone (they were barely invented then). But they have served as a basis for all sensory exploration, creativity, and wellbeing in my life. It was the best experience to develop creativity and a love and appreciation for nature. The quiet, the awareness of the sounds of the insects, the quality time with friends and the appreciation for the raw power of nature all gave me a deep respect and love for the natural world.

Though now my children are raised in a big city, I allow and encourage them at every chance to be outdoors and explore what is around us. We often go for bush walks together, and they are at the local park or playground weekly. Even into their teenage years they bike around the neighbourhood, exploring what is out there and creating their own experiences. Apart from the physical strength and development they gain, they also have time and space to themselves, and learn the limits and boundaries of their abilities. They can take measured risks and learn that fun and peace is always out there if they seek to discover it.

It is such memories that will form the foundation of their life experiences. They will carry with them what they have experienced and learned, and it will help them to form a character and belief system that is centered, balanced and respectful, as part of something larger.

I captured this photo at one of our local beaches. Being aware of the beauty that surrounds us is one of the best gifts you can give your children.

In addition to this, it must be mentioned that our children need time to explore the outdoors without supervision. This is done increasingly as they get older, but it is essential that it is done. Children need to learn how to take risks for themselves. How to feel appropriate amounts of fear and judge for themselves what the action should be. In modern life we tend to protect our children for longer than is necessary and this can be detrimental to their wellbeing. If we constantly make decisions for them, they will not be confident in making decisions on their own. If we constantly rescue them from difficult situations, then they will never build the resiliency to overcome challenges in life. These important traits are best formed in the natural environment where the laws of nature are predictable.

As our children take in the experiences of crashing waves or thunderous cicadas in a musty, tree-filled space, or as they feel soft sand and sharp rocks under their feet, they become aware of texture, sensation, where our body is in space, and how we should react in response to it.

The great thing about parenting is that in the early years your children look up to you and want to be just like you. If you enjoy it, you will do it, and your children will naturally follow you. For everyone out there who already makes the effort to be outside, touching, smelling, seeing, and enjoying the world around us—well done. You are already reaping all the benefits that outdoor exploration has to offer. The question then becomes, how else can you create new experiences?

DAD'S SAY

I'll be honest, I haven't always liked the outdoors – but I think that's only because my siblings and I weren't encouraged to be outside when we were children. We were allowed to play outside with our friends, but my parents didn't initiate or suggest that we spend time outside as a family. I still struggle to see the outdoors as relaxing. If there was a choice of movies or outdoors, my choice would be movies, but because I have learnt to see the benefits of the outdoors for my children and myself, such as the fresh air and moving, I am more often choosing to be outdoors.

I now know it's important for kids to be outdoors as this is part of their learning. I have encouraged my kids to play sports, and to have fun with their friends outside. The way I see it is the same as education: where some subjects are not enjoyed as much as others, but we still need them for everyday life.

Being outdoors builds confidence in learning new life skills such as through camping and walks. I had never been camping with my family when I was younger. However, my own family and I now try to go every year because I have seen how beneficial it is for the kids. They play outside, make new friends, learn new social skills, enjoy freedom and build memories. It is through these experiences that I am learning to see the outdoors as relaxing.

I have learnt compromise. If I do things that I enjoy with my kids, then we can all make the most of these opportunities. I choose to do this because I know that at the end of the day – my kids will win.

Ideas for Change

Here are 105 ways to play outside with your children at any age, and most of them are free!

1. Play with a hose

2. Sort leaves and flowers and make a scrapbook with them

3. Host a backyard campout: sleep outside under the stars, or in a tent

4. Have a bug hunt

5. Plant a garden

6. Build a hut

7. Start a nature scavenger hunt

8. Make crafts with boxes and glue

9. Have a waterslide

10. Buy a cheap camera and allow the kids to take photos

11. Provide toys that have to be used outdoors, such as Frisbees and balls

12. Do a full body painting on a huge sheet of paper

13. Go for a family bush walk

14. Melt some crayons in the sun

15. Play in a sandbox , or make one together if possible

16. Investigate the outdoors with a magnifying glass

17. Paint some rocks with water-based paints

18. Clean the car together (this one will help you out too!)

19. Hunt for "dinosaur" bones

20. Find crabs at the beach

21. Draw and then hose down some chalk letters and shapes

22. Ride a bike or scooter

23. Plant something (anything) in the garden

24. Harvest and taste what is in the garden

25. Mix some colours in water balloons then pop them on a board or wall

26. Play with a water table or make your own

27. Visit an animal sanctuary

28. Enjoy the local outdoor pools in summer

29. Take a ride on a ferry

30. Climb up a tree, a wall or a jungle gym

31. Make some bird feeders and feed the birds

32. Have a backyard toy wash

33. Pick some apples or fruit and have an impromptu snack under the trees

34. Spend some time on the swings

35. Visit a community garden and do some work to help out someone else

36. Go to a fairground or circus

37. Hunt for worms and slugs

38. Visit a wind farm if you have one in your area

39. Visit an outdoor farmers market

40. Go to a zoo

41. Have a family camping trip—you can't escape the outdoors there

42. Visit a racecourse

43. Go to the local playground (often!)

44. Explore playgrounds you have never been to

45. Make a nature collage of all the things you have found outside

46. Take a dog for a walk

47. Race some snails on paper

48. Pick a fresh bunch of flowers for a neighbour

49. Visit an old fashioned windmill

50. Make stepping stones for your garden

51. Go and visit an amphitheatre and get the kids to do some acting

52. Catch and release some frogs

53. Visit a cliff and look at the different types of rocks

54. Find a shallow river and work out how to cross it without getting wet

55. Go for a hike up a local mountain

56. Swim at the beach for the whole day

57. Colour the driveway with chalk

58. Play with a ball

59. Fish in a lake

60. Use a map and compass to scout out an island

61. Take some books outside and read under a tree

62. Go on a photo scavenger hunt

63. Spray paint something, e.g. furniture, canvas, old bikes

64. Do an egg and spoon race

65. Learn how to build an outdoor shelter—my boys love this

66. Visit a lighthouse, work out its height

67. Discover a new waterfall, swim if possible

68. Ride a horse

69. Visit a working farm

70. Feed sheep or horses

71. Visit an orchard and pick fruit, or a pick-your-own berry field

72. Trek through a local bush or forest and discover insects and animals native to your country

73. Plant a swan plant and watch for monarch caterpillars, chrysalises, and butterflies

74. Graffiti the driveway with washable paint

75. Stack and balance rocks

76. Have an ice cream taste test outside

77. Make the longest outdoor banana split

78. Go on a sound hunt and write down as many different sounds as you can

79. Make a treasure map and find treasure

80. Explore shells and rocks in rock pools

81. Make mud pies

82. Pick flowers and paint with them

83. Find shapes in the clouds

84. Host a mini Olympics with friends

85. Paint with water on the driveway and watch it evaporate

86. Sign up to an athletics club

87. Go on a tramping expedition and practise some overnight bush skills

88. Play cards on a mat outside

89. Go to a water garden or public garden and paint pictures of the flowers

90. Do the lawns and the garden together as a family

91. Hunt for river life and draw what you see

92. Feed eels in the local river or lake

93. Make the biggest sandcastle or join a competition

94. Body surf

95. Go to the local gardens and literally smell the roses!

96. Do a family bike ride together

97. Offer to help a neighbour clean up their back yard

98. Let older children pack themselves a lunch and go exploring on their bikes—by themselves!

99. Play 'spot the native bird' in your local bush

100. Lie in the long grass and listen to and feel your surroundings, practising mindfulness

101. Enjoy the late afternoon sun with a cold lemon water watching the shadows change

102. Roast marshmallows on an outdoor fire at night

103. Act out your favourite book outside, e.g. I'm Going on a Bear Hunt

104. Visit a historical building

105. Watch a sunset

Which ones will you implement this coming week?

TEACHER'S CORNER

Trying to implement a connection to nature in a classroom can be extremely difficult. With small classrooms, artificial outdoor spaces, and high child-to-teacher ratios, it can often be an uphill battle. However, even with the pressure to perform and reach standards and expectations in subjects and curriculum, a connection to nature needs to be at the forefront of our planning. We have a paramount opportunity to assist children who may never have had a significant connection to the outdoors and never learnt how it physically and mentally benefits us. Here are some ways that we can introduce and connect children to the outdoors through the classroom.

- Do an enquiry project or topic of lifecycles

- Set a project on creative sustainability

- Look at weather systems

- Ensure Learning Outside The Classroom (LOTC) trips are undertaken regularly to the outdoors

- Do a community focused project and tidy up a local river or park

- Learn about rubbish and where it goes

- Make end of term or year trips to natural playgrounds

- Think through disciplinary procedures; often children with negative behaviour need the outdoors the most

- Implement Nature Smart activities (Gardner's multiple intelligences)

- Plan and facilitate new experiences at break times and during PE and outdoor periods

- Ensure children come prepared for weather, with rain jackets and umbrellas

Impact on Wellbeing

Researchers are now finding that there is a difference not only in blood circulation, but also in the body's energy and brain functioning just from walking barefoot outside! So, it really isn't that far-fetched to accept that our own health, mood, thoughts and sense of peace can be improved by interacting with nature's energy.

Do you suffer from headaches? Feel stressed? Have high anxiety? Feel overwhelmed? I guarantee if you sit, stand, or lie outside on the grass, preferably around trees and plants, take five minutes to breathe deeply and become actively aware of your body and your surroundings, you will feel a change in your physiology. You will feel different. Utilising small strategies like this can be a huge help in our parenting journey. When you are overwhelmed and at the end of your tether, when your kids are winding you up, and you feel like you are going to explode, just stop. Walk outside. Breathe. And practice this, wherever you are.

I encourage you to just try it. Your physical, mental, emotional and spiritual health will benefit from it. Go somewhere beautiful, by yourself at first if you like, just explore your surroundings and focus on what is around you. Take the time to quiet your mind and observe what you can see and hear. Or do it with your children—even better. Help them learn how to become aware of their physical and emotional impulses and learn how to regulate them. Just ten minutes like this will convince you that spending time outdoors is not only great for children but is just as good for us as well. Give it a moment of thought now: how can you make the first step of getting outside?

Turning Teen

It is easy to picture our cute little toddlers, or cheeky seven year olds running through long grass or scaling rock walls. Often, as soon as that cuteness turns into a tween or teen, it can be hard to think of things to do with them, or how to motivate them, to be outdoors. Especially ideas that do not cost a lot of money.

My guiding principles of outdoor exploration for teens is to do what they have always loved but at a more challenging level. I remember when my two eldest boys were six and seven, we used to drive to different playgrounds to change things up and have some cheap fun. As they are very close in age they would often be competitive, challenging each other to do something, or showing each other how they could do it better.

One day we found a park that had a huge 'Spiderman' net. It was a triangular shaped concoction of ropes all intertwined for kids to climb up on. Getting to the top of that net was quite a feat for a six-year-old. Balance, hand-eye coordination, and bravery were all needed to scale it. My boys set off, each trying to be the quickest, and each trying to hide the nervousness they were really feeling. Well, maybe, it was me who was feeling the most nervous as I pictured the quickest route to the A&E!

It was a tall net and as they got to about half way I could see them slow down. They noticed just how far off the ground they were. They gripped a little bit tighter and looked at each other to see who was going to give up first. They never quite made it to the top that day. It was their first time and they weren't ready to take the risk.

Fast forward ten years and we have just had that very same experience with my teens and tweens. We were in the car together ready to go out when our plans were changed at the last minute. We discussed what we wanted to do, and we all agreed upon fish and chips at the park. I wondered to myself how long it would last. With no devices or games, with a lot of little kids around and everything at a kids' playground seemingly made for small children. But we gave it a go.

As soon as their food was finished, they were off. My big boys now, 6 ft 2" and just under 6 foot, were pushing

each other as they tried to balance on objects around them. That kept them amused for a lot longer than I thought it would, just as my younger two were running, swinging and climbing. They somehow all ended up on this net. The same kind of 'Spiderman' net that they played on all those years ago. I smiled as I saw the size of these boys. They could literally scale the thing in a few long strides.

No longer were they small and timid and unsure of their abilities. They were now confident, thrill-seeking, and risky.

Looking for ways to challenge themselves and play with danger. They all played tag together, and I watched as they ran around, jumped through, and balanced with no hands on the net.

In honesty, I couldn't believe how ecstatically happy they were. These big boys who are fighting for their independence, who are forging their way in the world, and who now tower over me. At heart, they are still those gorgeous little boys, wanting to have fun. And they found their own fun, even when I didn't think they would.

All I needed to do in this situation was make the most of an opportunity. Just do something weird and different and encourage them to get on board with it. There will always be some reluctance with this age group, but the more we can accommodate what they want, compromise, but continue to push for our family to be outdoors, the more we will all benefit.

I am proud that my children get along so well. They are considerate of others in these situations and they are each other's guardians. I would like to say it comes down to luck. But it doesn't. These values were intentionally taught, demonstrated, and discussed in our family throughout the years. And even though they squabble and fight like any other children, when it all comes down to it, this is who they are. Kind, considerate, caring, generous and playful children. The outdoors is the prime place to model and encourage these values in your children as they interact with their family, others, and nature.

Risk Taking

It has been proven over and again that children who learn how to take measured, appropriate risks in childhood will not participate as much in inappropriate risky behaviour when they are older (Sandsetter, 2011). Risky play also has other benefits, such as fostering problem solving, creating self management, competence and resilience (Greenfield, 2012). As mums, our instinct is to always protect our babies and prevent them from getting hurt. This is beautiful and natural, but we also need to balance that with measured risk.

Using the previous example of my six year old boys climbing the net - they instinctively knew their boundaries. They knew how far to climb before they didn't feel safe. They knew when to stop. If I had stopped them before they had reached their own limits, then they would never have had the opportunity to test and learn for themselves. Hopefully those opportunities will keep them from any truly stupid actions in the future that could cause them serious harm.

Sometimes, all we need to do is give our kids the freedom and opportunity to be, once again, in the outdoors, to see that they can enjoy it as teens.

The other way we can easily help our teens get off the couch and enjoy the outdoors is to invest in some toys. Big kids toys. The bucket and spade may no longer be of interest, but the kayak, paddle board or surfboard should definitely pique some interest. If they are not keen on the beach, then dirt bikes, trampolines, skateboards, horse riding or other risk-taking experiences help them to challenge themselves, learn their own boundaries, explore fun and enjoy life.

Maybe this week you can take your children outside and enjoy all that is out there. Breathe, connect, and rest. Try not to have too many expectations and you may be pleasantly surprised with how good you all feel afterwards.

'If I had stopped them then they would never have had the opportunity to test and learn for themselves.'

Action Points

What was your biggest 'Ah-ha!' moment of the outdoors chapter?

What are you immediately going to apply, change, or do now that you know this information?

What is your biggest barrier to being in the outdoors, and how can you overcome it?

Top Three Points to Ponder

- Being outdoors creates positive and long-lasting physical and structural changes in our brain that impact us positively—so go outside!

- Spending time outdoors, being physically active and eating well is essential for overall health, wellbeing, happiness, and academic achievement—so go outside!

- No matter what age your children are, you can always find different ways to enjoy being outside as a family. Set the example and lead courageously—so go outside!

'If we want our children to move mountains, we first have to let them get out of their chairs'.

~ **Nicolette Sowder**

L·O·V·E

Vestibular
Stimulation

V

Vestibular stimulation; physical movement

Vestibular Stimulation, n. of, relating to, or affecting the perception of body position and movement, the vestibular system of the inner ear.

Physical movement, adj. Physical activity is defined as any bodily movement produced by skeletal muscles that requires energy expenditure.

> *Understanding the science behind child development, the body-brain connection, learning through moving, developmentally appropriate practice, using the body to train the brain – increasing intelligence, embracing holistic development, bio-hacking.*

Why Movement?

I remember as a not-so-young kid, maybe a tween, walking to the park with my friend. We eagerly jumped on the swings and were laughing and swinging, competing with each other to go the highest, when I suddenly felt sick. Like, really sick. I slowed down, not wanting my friend to tease me, but I just couldn't keep on moving like that. Every time my legs swung trying to get higher and higher, my head whirred and my stomach felt like it was in my throat. I wanted to run behind the bush and vomit. Even after I had stopped and sat on a seat, I still felt ill. My friend seemed to be enjoying it and was thrilled that she was going higher than me (she loved the feeling of butterflies in her stomach), but I knew I couldn't keep going. I decided from that point on to avoid swings at any cost.

However, that motion sickness still managed to find me. For instance, when a friend and I were heading off to school camp. The place we were staying was a good 1.5 hours away. We packed up, excited and chatting, thrilled to be going together. That was until I was in her car and realised her window wouldn't go down all the way. I knew this spelled danger for me.

We were barely 40 minutes out of our little town when the nausea and throbbing head started. I tried to breathe, tried to chew, doing all the things I had learned to combat this feeling, but they were useless. Within ten minutes I received a good telling-off for being sick in the back of my friend's mum's car. Talk about embarrassing! Unfortunately, I hadn't wanted to slow her down and had instead tried to contain it, but I just couldn't. Honestly, no one wants to be THAT kid! Maybe this was you, too? Maybe this is one of your kids? I now know why this happens and how we can help it.

What I didn't realise then, but do know now, was that my vestibular system was under-developed and it showed itself in those symptoms—motion sickness, car sickness, unease with heights. I just lived with it, I was just 'that kid'. I stayed away from swings, tried not to go on long car trips, avoided heights, and quite honestly just wished I didn't have this problem. No one wants to feel like that! Even as an adult I have embarrassingly had motion sickness, and yes even with the pills that are supposed to stop it. It's not exactly fun, and it can limit the things you do and places you go.

Our Modern Society

As a modern society we have developed an obsession with sitting still. The games and devices that are currently on trend usually mean children are sitting still to engage with them. When children are at school they are expected to sit still most of the time, not utilising the power of the body to train the mind. When children are in lessons outside of school, they usually have to sit. Then you add on all the routine things such as eating, driving, and of course watching TV, where we are always...you guessed it—sitting.

Have you ever stopped and added up the sitting hours you or your children do in a day? No wonder many children are labelled with Attention Deficit Hyperactivity Disorder (ADHD) from a young age. For many of them, they are simply expected to keep still a lot longer than is developmentally appropriate for them. Children need to move, it's how we are wired. Jumping, twisting, turning, running, rolling, walking, crawling, moving. Most of our children would benefit from more movement especially in the early and middle years.

The current minimum level of exercise recommended by the New Zealand Ministry of Health (2018) is at least one hour per day for children and young people. This is the minimum, but often we struggle to maintain even this small amount.

Our desire for convenience has nearly outweighed our conscience when it comes to our health and how we move our bodies. The scary thing is, this will be the norm for a lot of children's lives growing up. We tend to choose what is easy rather than what is best. A practical way of combatting this is to set boundaries with time on devices. Once the rules are established, it is just a matter of ensuring we consistently enforce them. If children don't have anything to do, it is my experience that they usually create their own fun. Playing and moving isn't work to them—it's fun.

The Vestibular System Explained

What does the Vestibular component of L.O.V.E really stand for? Is it only movement? Something we presume is generally normal for childhood? Not quite. All movement is good and beneficial for our bodies and can release the right neurochemicals in our brain to help us feel good and sleep well, adults and children alike, but not all movement is equal.

Our vestibular system is the first sensory system developed when we are in the womb. It is located inside our ear and it gives us our sense of balance and tells us when and how we are moving. Have you ever had vertigo or motion sickness? That is your vestibular system telling your brain that you are moving when your eyes are telling your brain you are not. The brain gets two different messages and can't quite distinguish which one is correct—the outdoors flying by or the inside of the car being still? This is the power of the vestibular system.

What happens when children don't get the movement they need? Unfortunately, there are tragic stories of this occurring in our time. Some of the saddest examples of this can be seen in orphanages around the world. Small, undernourished and impoverished children, barely able to walk and talk, with stunted physical growth and huge emotional problems, show us all too well how important movement is to a growing and developing body and brain (Pappas, 2012).

How will these children have a chance at a prolonged and fulfilling life with so much neglect in the beginning? It's heart wrenching and completely preventable. The lack of movement, attachment, physical and verbal interaction become huge blocks to language, motor and social development. Children can be developmentally years behind their chronological age with little chance of ever catching up.

'Therefore intelligence—especially in the earlier years—relies heavily on the movement of the body'.

This is an extreme example but one that demonstrates just how much our development relies on movement. From sensory perception to expressive language and physiological progression, it all begins with movement. I cannot overstate how important movement is for our children. They need to be off the couch and moving. Sure, having them quietly babysat by the TV may be convenient, but it is not helping them.

We rarely hear about the vestibular system and its huge importance in physical development, let alone academic learning. It is our vestibular system that will determine our physical coordination and balance. Every kind of learning relies on our physical processing of information. For example, standing still with our eyes closed is the highest and hardest form of balance as it relies on your vestibular system to process exactly where you are in relation to gravity and everything else around you without any support from your eyes.

You try it. Stand still with your feet together and eyes closed. Slowly count to 30. Did you move, wobble, or sway? Did you feel like you were moving even if you weren't physically moving?

Now try it with your child. Have them stand with feet together and eyes closed and slowly count up to ten. Even in those short seconds I am sure you will see them wobble and move. If they are over seven, count to 30. This will test their vestibular systems and you will see just how finely tuned it is. Swaying and moving means that it is not as finely tuned as it should be, and for school, sports and life it really needs to be.

Movement is Learning

Movement IS the foundation of all learning and this doesn't stop at any age. Our physical potential is limitless. Every sense and perception we have comes through movement. Our body is constantly moving to process information. When we read, our eyes are moving. When we think, chemicals and electromagnetic waves are moving inside our brains. When we learn a sport, our body is moving and our brain is training our muscles to move in a specific pattern. To speak, our mouths and tongue are working. To write our hands, fingers and arms are moving with support from our posture.

There is no perception or learning that occurs without movement (Goddard Blythe, 2005). Can you think of one? Even ideas are created by the firing of neurons in the brain. Yet in our society, the body is rarely thought of in relation to intelligence or learning and it is definitely underutilised.

Therefore intelligence—especially in the earlier years—relies heavily on the movement of the body. The simple equation is 'movement = learning'. No movement, no learning. The impact of this is so far reaching that doctor's and scientists now agree that we can prevent dementia and Alzheimer's disease through specific movement (Alzheimers Association, 2019). If that isn't enough motivation, I have more!

There is never a time where we don't need to move. Our bodies are wired to be at optimal health and performance mentally, physically, and emotionally when we are getting enough movement. The body trains the brain. Our bodies and brains are intricately connected. I am not sure why as a society, we began to separate each component out and think we only needed to develop children's brains.

A fun memory of my three boys and their friends, playing rugby on a sunny summer's day in Auckland.

The complexities of our bodies are amazing! I truly marvel at the design and ability of our physical systems and the intricate ways they work together. When we look at our little babies and see their perfection, how can we not be amazed? They don't try to breathe, grow or develop—they just do. Our physical bodies are immensely powerful in that just by moving repetitively they can create and form new neural connections in the brain. Wow. We can change, grow and form our children's brains through movement. That is a super empowering thought! It is from this curiosity, and my desire to do the best for my children that I embarked on the journey of discovering how we can enhance our brain functioning, learning, behaviour, intelligence and overall success. I am pleased to be able to share some of what I have learned here.

Movement and Neuro-Motor Immaturity

For children who cannot sit or stand still and are always on the go (the ones that always operate at full speed throughout the day), it is most likely that their vestibular system is underdeveloped. There can be many causes of an underactive or overactive vestibular system. One of these causes is in relation to how much movement experience the child has received in the first year of life. Another is the health of Mum and child during the pregnancy, and there are other environmental factors as well.

We may never know why these things are the way they are, and in many cases it can be out of our control. But we do know that it doesn't have to stay that way. There are ways to help develop the vestibular system, and ways to ensure our children's movement is helping them and not hindering them.

There are specific movement patterns that all neurotypical, physically able children should be making in their first year of life. These should come naturally and without effort if the child has experienced enough free movement time and if there haven't been any other medical issues hindering their development. They will learn to wriggle and roll, sit and crawl, and eventually stand and walk. These initial actions stem from automatic movements called primitive reflexes. As babies we don't think about moving in such ways, it just comes naturally. Primitive reflexes are quite easy to understand: it is a movement that happens without having to think of doing it.

KEY: NEURO = BRAIN MOTOR = MOVEMENT

A well-known example of this is the 'Palmer grasp'. If you place your finger into a newborn's hand, what happens? Their fingers will close around your finger and grasp onto it. This is a primitive reflex. They control the baby's body in the first year of life because their brain is not developed enough to think rationally or cognitively about what to do. It allows them to breathe their first breath (Moro Reflex) and also helps them keep their airway free in their first months (The Asymmetrical Tonic Neck reflex, [ATNR]). There are many other functions that the different reflexes perform, and the common thread is that they are all automatic stereotyped movements controlled by our brain stem (Goddard Blythe, 2005). That means they happen without us thinking about it. These primitive reflexes should last for a short time and then be 'put to sleep' so that postural reflexes can develop. Postural reflexes are the reflexes that we have as adults. They help us stand upright against gravity and produce coordinated and synchronous movements.

Our postural reflexes should be fully developed by the time we are four years old, however in my experience in teaching and with individual clients, many children still have their primitive reflexes at age four and above—even though these should no longer be active after one year of age.

'NMI occurs when the brain and the body are still communicating in an immature way, using the 'baby' brain rather than the 'adult' brain'.

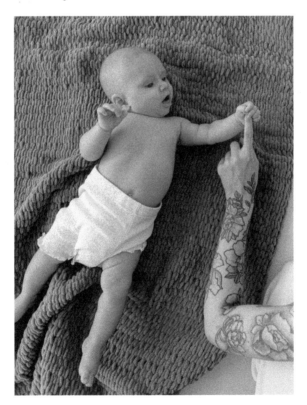

An image of the Palmer grasp. Cute when they are a few weeks old, but detrimental when they are trying to learn to write.

Postural reflexes allow us to form mature and complex patterns of movement without having to think about it. When postural reflexes are fully developed they also stop the primitive reflexes being triggered. This means we are able to continually operate in our 'adult' rational and cognitive brain by choice rather than our 'baby' brain taking over. How naturally a child moves their body is a good indicator of Neuro-Motor Immaturity [NMI].

NMI occurs when the brain and the body are still communicating in an immature way using the 'baby' brain rather than the 'adult' brain. If the brain hasn't finished its early development within the first year of life this can cause the child to still be 'switched' back into their baby brain. This is an absolute pain for kids in the classroom! Children often struggle with focus and concentration because their bodies are constantly interrupting their brain processes.

Therefore, when a child still has active primitive reflexes past four years of age, this shows the level of immaturity in their central nervous system [CNS] (Goddard Blythe, 2009). It is a warning signal that their central nervous system, which connects and communicates information between the body and the brain, is underdeveloped. This, if not remedied, will lead to further difficulties in the years to come. Our central nervous system influences behaviour, emotion, coordination, balance and attention. It is our most foundational system. If these primitive reflexes are still present beyond the first year of life, or if there are underdeveloped postural reflexes after four years old, this indicates neuro motor immaturity (Goddard Blythe, 2005), and a range of painful behaviours will follow. This is why movement is key in those first few years of life.

'Children often struggle with focus and concentration because their bodies are constantly interrupting their brain processes'.

You will see these symptoms even if you don't know the cause. In everyday life these reflexes frustrate children, and the resulting behaviour, immaturity, learning difficulties and meltdowns frustrate their parents and teachers. But most importantly, they make the child's life very hard. They can have problems with attention, balance, focus, movement, mid-line crossing, fine motor skills (e.g. pencil holding and handwriting), emotional self-regulation, outbursts, speech difficulties, problems with numbers and directions, and the list goes on. The underlying cause of these problems, and even some of the symptoms of Autism and ADHD, is that the child still has primitive reflexes present when they shouldn't have. Research has shown that there are now links between retained primitive reflexes and children diagnosed with these issues (Goddard Blythe, 2005).

The good news however, is that there are ways to overcome Neuro-Motor Immaturity! By using a specific movement programme which gives the child's brain a second chance of forming the connections it should have in the first year of life, we can put primitive reflexes to sleep, develop postural reflexes and mature the child's central nervous system. But to prevent it in the first place, the child must get as much varied free movement time in their first four years of life as possible. The brain is amazing; it knows what needs to happen. It uses the body to do it. When we repeat all those specific movement patterns that occur in the first year of life we help alleviate NMI.

🔑 In schools and preschools NMI can be remediated through a specific programme that is aimed to meet the needs of the general school population. It is conducted five days a week in schools, with pre- and post-assessments to measure progress. Teachers can be trained in the use of this programme and then implement it in their classroom. It takes just fifteen minutes per day and doesn't need any expensive equipment. There has been a lot of research conducted in the UK on the success of the programme, and more is to come in other countries. For more information see withoutlimitslearning.com.

🔑 NMI also has links to Sensory Processing Disorder [SPD]. The central nervous system is responsible for communicating information from our senses to our brain. Therefore, an immaturity in this system will mean the information is not being understood properly. Problems will be seen in sensitivity to loud noises, light, tactile aversion, hypersensitive skin and eating difficulties to name a few. Many primitive reflexes cause the same symptoms. Teachers have an amazing opportunity to introduce a variety of sensory activities to their students throughout the school day, as well as a reflex programme. By maturing the central nervous system through a reflex remediation programme many sensory problems will diminish. Seek to ensure that your school day is filled with fun, new and interesting activities that create a sense of awe. The brain loves novelty and will remember information and experiences better when this occurs. Ensure you make use of the whole body, and the child will retain more of the content you are trying to teach.

Ensure you give your children 'Brain Breaks'. These are key times where children can allow different brainwaves to occur, release built up energy and tension and use other parts of their brains. Structure your day to include a range of movement activities, talking time, quiet time, and new experiences to enhance your students' work flow.

IQ, EQ, and MQ?

We are uniquely intertwined and connected—our bodies, minds, emotions and spirits—that it is near impossible for any system to act in isolation to another. We are complex creatures, and I know if we can see our children's growth as more than academic learning then we will begin to tap into the intricate power of our being. We must allow our children a natural childhood, one where each and every aspect of their development is understood. One where they learn and are taught in a holistic way. If all aspects of their development are recognised and nurtured; body, brain, emotions and spirit, then we will truly be setting our children up for success. If their IQ, EQ, and MQ along with their spiritual development is also developed, enhanced and supported, our children will grow into the well-rounded conscientious adults we desire them to be. Let me break down some of these terms further.

We need to see a Natural Childhood Movement (#thenaturalchildhoodmovement) established, where parents, teachers and professionals join together to change the course of our education, parenting and social systems to put the holistic development of our children first. This movement will encourage the adults that daily work with children to continue to provide the most natural environments possible, developing their vestibular and proprioceptive systems so that they will develop efficient and mature movement patterns. The movement aims to ensure parents and teachers are directly involved with developing children's emotional resilience and nurturing their confidence. If we take intentional action and practical steps towards this, encouraging and supporting other adults on their own journeys, we can change the course of society to one where we support children to be their natural best. Let's band together to make this natural childhood movement a reality. The status quo is usually the path of least resistance, but if we all encourage one other person and make one small change, we can make this a reality.

Most of us know what IQ is or represents. It is Intelligence Quotient, or as we would generally think of it, how brainy we are. An intelligence quotient (IQ) is a total score derived from several standardized tests designed to assess human intelligence. The abbreviation "IQ" was coined by the psychologist William Stern, from the German term Intelligenzquotient. This was Stern's term for a scoring method for intelligence tests undertaken at University of Breslau, which he advocated in a 1912 book. (Intelligence Quotient, 2019). Historically, an IQ is a score obtained by dividing a person's mental age (obtained by administering an intelligence test), by the person's chronological age, both expressed in terms of years and months. The resulting fraction is multiplied by 100 to obtain the IQ score. About two-thirds of the population scores are between IQ 85 and IQ 115. About 2.5 percent of the population scores above 130, and 2.5 percent below 70. Though now, many people do not carry out the actual IQ test, IQ has become the term for intelligence, braininess, or academic success.

'The Natural Childhood Movement is about encouraging the holistic development of children; mind, body, emotions and spirit, and keeping this holistic development at the forefront of our parenting, teaching and learning'.

Just as we consider IQ or intelligence of high importance, as we encourage and support our children to 'reach for the stars' and achieve excellence in academic subjects, we need to see all aspects of their development esteemed, supported and rewarded.

EQ or Emotional Quotient (emotional intelligence) has been shown to be a key indicator of future success in careers. There is now just as much evidence showing that how children learn to empathise and relate to others throughout childhood determines their opportunities and future professional success as adults. Emotional resilience is just as important as intelligence. A quick search on Google will show how this is fast becoming recognised as the leading requirement in job applications, recruitment and appraisals. It is a term popularised by science journalist Coleman (2008), and is described as 'the capability of individuals to recognise their own emotions and those of others, discern between different feelings and label them appropriately, use emotional information to guide thinking and behaviour, and manage and/or adjust emotions to adapt to environments or achieve one's goal(s)'.

The other aspect of our intelligence however, and one that gets little discussion, is a child's movement ability. In my experience, the way a child moves indicates what is happening in their brain. I suggest that if we measure anything, we really should be measuring their development of movement, or their Movement Quotient [MQ]. This term can be used to describe a person's movement ability and the subsequent implications on other areas of development. The function of this term is to allow equal priority to the role and development of our bodies and how we use them and increase understanding of how the movement of the body indicates and enhances the maturity of brain pathways. Yes, it is possible to be highly intelligent (IQ) and in some ways be slightly uncoordinated or potentially a little emotionally immature. However, is this the holistic development we want for our children? By developing a child's MQ, their IQ and EQ will also increase.

Therefore, the ability to move precisely, efficiently and with unconscious control is foundational for thinking, learning and emotional development. We need to move away from the thought that 'my child is intelligent if they get the top grades, win the spelling bee, and are chosen for the accelerant classes'. There are many more forms of intelligence and they all need to be recognized. Academic, emotional and movement intelligence – they all have their place.

To summarise, The Natural Childhood Movement is about encouraging the holistic development of children; mind, body, emotions and spirit, and keeping this holistic development at the forefront of our parenting, teaching and learning. Ensuring that as societies we develop ways where this lifestyle can be maintained and improved in the years to come.

Self-help guru, Tony Robbins has said that 'Physiology affects psychology'. How we move our body affects what is happening in our minds and we can change what is going on in our minds by changing what is happening with our body. Wow! Think about that for a moment. We can help children to change their thinking by changing what their body is doing. It is simple yet powerful.

As teachers we are not required to study papers on neuroscience, and even more alarming is that there is very little training on how to utilise children's physical states to enhance the learning process either. It has largely been left to the private sector to educate teachers in this area. My training in neurodevelopmental therapy has changed the course of my teaching career. I look at children in a new light and understand why a lot of their behaviour is occurring. I can see how they move in a playground and get a pretty good idea of what is happening in their brains. Play time isn't only for relaxation, it is just as essential as class time. We can use movement as a tool to get the best out of them.

I encourage every teacher to explore this area. Read more, educate yourself, and implement different strategies. You will never regret it. In addition to this, I suggest that we need to think through our disciplinary policies, and any strategies that take children's play times away as punishment. It is my experience that the children who misbehave the most are the ones who need the free outdoor play time the most. Every child has a right to play, and there are more effective ways, ones that can benefit the child and the teacher alike, than taking away outdoor movement time.

Ways to recognize neuro motor immaturity in the classroom:

- Poor balance

- Delay in motor milestones - uncoordinated bilateral movements

- Floppy or overly rigid head control

- Continuous verbal and physical movements (overflow)

- Poor muscle tone – floppy child

- Inability to mentally rotate and reverse objects in space (e.g. time on a clock, symmetrical shapes)

- Cannot work out how to do certain physical activities (e.g. push and pull)

- Dislike of heights (e.g. swings and roundabouts)

- Difficulties with spatial awareness, physically or on paper

- Difficulty sitting still (e.g. seeking vestibular stimulation through rocking and spinning)

- Clumsiness

- Poor sense of direction both on paper and in person

- Sloping handwriting

- Hit first, think later child

- Emotional meltdowns

- Selective mutism (in some cases)

- Sensory averse or seeking

- Lying on the desk, often holding head, with paper slanted

Developing a Vestibular-Strong Child

I know it can be hard reading through all the technical jargon and still being sure of what you need to do. Don't worry. I offer practical tools and ways to help your child in this book. You will finish this book feeling empowered! Remember, if you have bought this book, you care. You are interested in your child's development and you want what is best for them. You are halfway there already—trust me. A caring, proactive parent is what every child needs.

This principle of vestibular stimulation, or movement, works well with the outdoors principle and embodies the Natural Childhood Movement. Growing children holistically, these principles operate together—intertwined just as our minds, bodies, and spirits are. When children move outdoors they are not only gaining natural energy, but creating physiological changes in the brain due to movement of the body. For example, the balance system is fully functioning at 16 weeks after conception and is active at birth. It responds to movement (especially slow movement) over a range of planes. This occurs when the head is tilting side to side, forwards and backwards, or rotating around (Goddard Blythe, 2011). We can use this knowledge to then support our children to gain this particular movement experience and do it in the outdoors. Swinging, and hanging upside down on playgrounds is a great way to support your child's vestibular development.

Now don't start panicking about a massive life change. The change will come when you answer the smaller questions of what, where, and when. Truly, just start small. Think of what you are doing now in the area of movement and choose one thing more. Use parks, playgrounds and pools that are close by and then expand to other areas, or go more often, or just stay a bit longer. You may think that your toddler isn't learning much from climbing the ladder and sliding down the slide, over and over again. But even after the hundredth time, they are—absolutely. We also learn patience, don't we? When we recognise the value in what they are doing it is much easier to encourage them.

As my first two children are less than two years apart I constantly felt like I was running after one or the other. I remember being at the playground, having to watch every direction at once, because they were both such a handful. Two boys under three—and it wasn't long after I had another child on the way!

Needless to say, I know how you feel. I know what you are going through when your brain cries out for adult conversation and demands to know how long you are going to have to stand at this slide. I remember the feelings of frustration, and quite frankly, just being fed up with it all. The routine, the nappies, the mess, the despair of saying something 100 times and then having to say it one more.

Yes, those younger years are tough, but looking back, I don't have a single regret. I don't regret giving my children my time, my body, my love, or even that one last push on the swing. It is these small things that we will treasure as time goes on. It is these daily deposits into their lives that will bring out all their inner potential and goodness—even if we don't see it when they are teens! One last swing, one last slide. I encourage you to do it for them, knowing you are building their brain power, their social skills and their bodies.

These days I don't have to get as physically involved anymore. I had a small blessing when our internet wouldn't work and because of this no one could do homework. The 15-, 13-, and 11-year-old devised to make their own game out on the back deck with balls, skateboards and challenges. No one told them to do it. I didn't create the game, but I am thankful that this has become their go-to when they have nothing to do. They just get together and play.

Yes it's noisy, yes, sometimes things get broken, and yes, there are disagreements to mediate. But because I see the immense value to their bodies, brains, spirits, as well as their social skills, I don't stop them. If you create this habit and put in the time when they are younger, I know your children will do the same. As we train them and set their 'normality' during their younger years they will continue that way when they are older. What do you want your kids normal to be?

Doing things together with our children and encouraging movement as much as possible will provide them with the habit of moving. It creates a normality for their future. How do you want them to be when they are older? Do you want them to exercise regularly and eat healthily? Then it is those things we need to do with them from the moment they are born. If you move and play with them then they will move and play on their own. They will see themselves as living, moving beings, and when they move it will reinforce all the joy and curiosity they feel as well as creating all the positive brain chemicals (e.g. dopamine). It's a win-win for them and it shows that this is what life is like—this is normal. By adopting this lifestyle consistently our children will subconsciously understand how clever their bodies are and how they can be used.

I can't stress enough the importance of regularly and consistently getting kids to move their bodies. This is how they will live their future lives, and in turn, raise their own children. Start young and carry on all the way through, or better yet just start today. It's never too late.

Swings are a great source of vestibular stimulation but can cause discomfort if a child has an underdeveloped vestibular system.

Maybe you have been to the park every day for the last week, and you cannot bear to think of going again. The saying that 'variation is the spice of life' is poignantly true and just as relevant when we are trying to get our children to move. As adults we like to play sports or try different activities and our children are the same.

If we do the same thing all the time we are not challenging ourselves physically or mentally. Have you ever committed to a new exercise routine? It's super fun and motivating in the beginning, isn't it? But by week three or four our brain goes, 'not again!' It is the same for our children. While all movement is good, there are ways that we can introduce more challenging forms of movement to keep them motivated and offer the body and brain new ways of developing. The brain does need a certain amount of repetition. The brain is lazy in that it likes everything to be routine and on 'automatic pilot'. This is why children repeat things over and over when they are younger. When something becomes automatic it can be performed as you are doing something else, or without conscious thought. Once the brain has formed that automatic connection, even the slightest variation can make the same activity fun and enjoyable again.

For example, when children can jump with two feet together and in time, encourage them to try hopping on one, like hopscotch. Again, look for mastery, balance and rhythm, and then encourage them to hold something in their hands while hopping. Then see if they can do it backwards. If they master this and still need further expansion, then they can jump longer, or wider, or over something. But wait, there is still more you can do with just this one simple activity! You can challenge them to jump with two feet, then one, then two, and create routines with alternating feet and jumps to offer them something new. You can make a friendly competition out of it, or offer a prize. This is just one example of ways we can play with our children without them even knowing they are developing their bodies and brains! Our only limitation is our imagination.

'While all movement is good, there are ways that we can introduce more challenging forms of movement to keep them motivated and offer the body and brain new ways of developing'.

It doesn't matter what the activity is; when children learn something and then attempt a harder way of doing it, they develop more neural connections and problem solving abilities. By expanding their activities, you create and maintain new neurological pathways (the neurons and synapses required for fast processing of information). Imagine that, just by moving we are encouraging intelligence! This may have been the best-kept secret of childhood, and now this power is in your hands.

I want to lay out a challenge to give your children free moving time every day. Start by observing what they love to do, the things they do over and over again, then create a way to make it better. If they are old enough, they can walk themselves to the park, meet new friends and challenge their physical boundaries. Or if they aren't old enough yet, allow them time in the back yard.

They could create obstacle courses, challenges, or sports games so they are interested and engaged in the play they are doing. Of course, it is great if you are there engaging with them in the activities they are doing, but this isn't always possible. Remember, by allowing your children the freedom to explore their physical limitations on their own, within safe boundaries, you are strengthening their independence, resilience, and decision making ability. There is immense value physically and psychologically in this process.

Did you know that from the moment of conception the child's body is moving? Movement is that natural. All we really need to do is offer our children the time and space, and every now and then, the resources, and they will do the rest. Of course, as they get older, we can get resistance from our children. Anyone with a child who is two can testify to that! Rather than giving into the demands of our children to be entertained we can maintain their space for imaginative free play. In this way, we don't overly structure, burden or force what they do. As busy modern parents we really don't need more work to do, therefore encourage your kids to have choice in what they do and make it lots of fun! This will help your children to take the lead. It's about engaging them in the process, asking for their thoughts and opinions, and then giving them the feeling that they have power over the decisions being made. This encourages them to buy into the process by giving them a voice, giving them new options, and giving them a way to create their own ideas.

DAD'S SAY

Being a Pacific Islander, my identity is rooted in my culture. I was brought up with certain rules and a couple come to mind when I think about moving and learning. One of these rules was, there is no playing on Sunday. Another was, there is no running/yelling/laughing loudly in the house.

All we did on a Sunday was come home from church and sleep. It was a day of rest. Even if it was sunny outside with blue skies, and even as little kids, we were not allowed to play.

In the beginning of our marriage and family, this was my own personal mindset about Sundays' and it took a lot to change my mind on this point, because I had never seen it any other way. But moving forward, being married to Leanne and living in a different era, our life is completely different.

My eldest son has dance practice on Sundays and is at a professional level. If I stayed in the same mindset that I used to have, I honestly don't think that he would be where he is or have the success he has. I am glad that I have faced and worked through this mental block, because I am now encouraging and supporting of my children's active play—even on a Sunday!

I have come to learn that all kids want to be physical. They all need to move and they are usually better behaved when they do. I'll admit, I don't have the same passion for movement that my wife does, and yet we make it work. As a dad, I feel the need to build more traditions in our lives that include movement such as camps, overseas trips and family walks and then be consistent about it. This is easier said than done after a grueling work week. But brainstorming ideas together now that our children are older, and including them in the decisions, helps us all to enjoy our time moving about.

Ideas for Change

If you have a newborn baby you can develop their vestibular system by keeping them closely connected to you physically from the time they are born. This not only forms a strong attachment between the two of you (as we learnt in the first chapter), but also develops their awareness of movement. Whether they are being held or strapped, it doesn't really matter as either method will develop their vestibular and sensory systems. Day-to-day activities can become a world of newness for an infant when an adult walks around with them. Their brain will learn about movement, their eyes will develop and they will be exposed to different sounds and senses.

You can use simple tasks such as holding your child, lying them down and picking them back up to stimulate their vestibular system and help develop their proprioception system (understanding where they are in relation to other things). The movement, force and pull of

PROPRIOCEPTION

Proprioception enables us to know where parts of our body are at any time even if we are not consciously thinking about it. Our proprioceptive system will communicate to our vestibular system to make any changes to maintain our balance.

The proprioceptors in our nerve endings send information to the brain about the amount of flexion, tension and stretch our muscles, ligaments and tendons need.

The proprioceptive system also communicates to our vestibular system.

gravity awakens their vestibular system and exposes them to new sensations. As the vestibular is the first system being developed it is essential to move them during this time.

Through the first few months of life primitive reflexes play their biggest role. When a baby is able to lie on their tummy they will gradually gain control over their head movements. Their development begins with the head and moves down the body to the other limbs and the core before they have control over the arms and legs and eventually fingers and toes. Once they have mastered tummy time they will learn to wiggle and roll over. These movements are reflexes, just like the ones that help the baby sit up and eventually crawl, so it's important to give them a lot of free moving space on the floor at this time.

As soon they can get into a 'hands and knees' position, they will rock and start trying to crawl. There are many different views on crawling, but it is essential! Encourage, help and support your child to crawl. Many children with NMI have not crawled long enough or at all as babies. There have also been links between the continued presence of primitive reflexes and children with ADHD (Konicarova, Bob & Raboch, 2013). This again proves that the mind is embodied. The body is a powerful trainer of the mind. Crawling is the beginning training of bilateral movements—that is opposite hand to knee/leg working together. These kinds of movements form connections between the right and left hemispheres in the brain, and through repetition these connections are strengthened. This becomes the basis for all movement we do as adults.

When older children cannot move fluidly, it is often because of a lack of crawling as well. Crawling is key to development, therefore, if you child wants to stand up too quickly, I suggest you play floor games and help them enjoy the crawling process more. This is because by crawling the body is integrating and developing specific reflexes. If the child cannot crawl properly, it suggests primitive reflexes are still very strong and the brain has not developed more mature connections.

Once your child can walk, life gets interesting! They are usually off in a hurry and want to touch anything and everything in their path. Keeping them safe at this time is key, but the more they can run and walk, the more they will learn and the more the motor area of their brain will develop. Gross motor movement (large muscles such as arms and legs) must develop before fine motor movement can (fingers, toes, eyes). The brain does a lot of 'pruning' which means it cuts off any neural pathways that aren't being used. In order to have a lot of connections or neural pathways within your child's brain, specific pathways must be used again and again until the repetition fuses neurons and dendrites together and strengthens it. This creates a new skill and pathway allowing

GROSS MOTOR

Gross motor (physical) skills are those which require whole body movement and which involve the large (core stabilising) muscles of the body to perform everyday functions, such as standing and walking, running and jumping, and sitting upright at the table. They also include hand-eye coordination skills such as ball skills (throwing, catching, and kicking) as well as riding a bike or a scooter and swimming.

messages to travel across. Neuro science is a fascinating and intricate subject that can teach us a lot about how to best support our children.

There are many movement games, rhymes and actions that also support physical growth over the early years. Many that you probably remember your parents doing with you! You can put children on your knee and 'ride horse', teach them to roly poly, wrestle with young children, use massage, and play finger rhymes (Where is Thumbkin). In addition to strengthening movement patterns, language will develop and they will be able to communicate their wants as well. These kinds of games develop the child's vestibular system, proprioceptive system, language acquisition, long term memory, predictive skills and executive functioning as well as much more!

Thinking of our modern society and things that hinder our children's development, there are specific practices that aren't beneficial when used in excess. Our busy lives usually mean we take baby from the cot to high chair to the car seat to the play pen to the high chair and so on.

Being aware and conscious of how much time our babies get to move is the first step in setting them up for success. When we stop children's movement, we are also stopping their cognitive development – plain and simple. Practically we can avoid propping and sitting up our baby before they are ready. Those little plastic chairs may look cute, but it doesn't help our children's development because they don't yet have the muscle control for it. We will know when they are ready to sit because they will have strong enough muscles to keep themselves in a sitting position on their own. But if we do this too often before they are ready, it can do more harm than good.

It is the exploration of movement in this crucial time frame that will give the child's brain the ability to know where they are in space and to control their movements by choice rather than by reflex. Think through all the equipment you use with a baby. Bouncers and jolly jumpers may be giving some movement experiences for short periods of time, but how long are they in cots, chairs, capsules, walkers etc.?

Here are some movement ideas by age group. It's by no means a definitive list, but just a place to start (you can find some of the rhymes at the back of the book):

> **ENCOURAGING MOVEMENT**
>
> 1. Observe what they are doing
>
> 2. Allow exploration
>
> 3. Provide a deeper level of interaction
>
> 4. Do it in the context of love, attachment and acceptance

Ages 0 – 1

Physical connection to you

1. Strap your newborn baby to you as you move around doing chores.

2. Lie on your back with baby's tummy on top of your tummy and talk and play games.

3. Put your baby on a mat on their tummy or back. As they get older put interesting objects around them so they can reach for them.

4. Do baby massage, with gentle pressure on the whole body. If you sing or say the body parts, you are also supporting new language skills.

5. While talking to your baby, move their arms and legs for them and laugh and smile. Action rhymes are perfect for this.

6. Allow your baby as much space as possible on the floor for safe exploration.

7. Encourage the forward-backward rocking movement on hands and knees they make before crawling.

8. Get down and crawl with them, chasing and playing.

9. Help your baby stand when they are ready and be patient when they begin to walk.

10. Give your baby tons of cuddles, love, books, and songs.

11. Enjoy the outdoors as much as possible, verbalising what you see.

Ages 1 – 3

Physical connection to the world

1. Move as much as possible, doing follow-the-leader games, action rhymes etc.

2. Play Peek-a-Boo or Jack in the Box.

3. Have bunny hopping races, frog races and any other races.

4. Catch bubbles, balls and other objects.

5. Use music and instruments to dance and sing and explore rhythm and timing.

6. Play hopscotch, focusing on jumping with two feet together and then extending.

7. Act like different animals and move and speak like they would.

8. Use a giant parachute to move over, under and around.

9. Throw bean bags or toys or anything into buckets and hoops.

10. Visit places such as the zoo or an aquarium.

Ages 3 – 6

Physical connection to others

1. Play What's the Time Mr Wolf, Hot Potato or larger group games.

2. Balance poses—copy me, e.g. one leg stand, triangle, rectangle etc.

3. Tightrope walking on a balance beam or line on the ground.

4. Follow-the-leader games, or hopping and running races with other children.

5. Difficult obstacle courses exploring over, under, in, on, and through.

6. Gymnastics class or at home, e.g. roly-poly, beams and spinning, hanging, swiss ball.

7. Different throwing styles (over- and under-arm) with different sized balls from different distances, encouraging and developing catching.

8. Climbing activities at playgrounds or in trees.

9. Swimming, paddling and supervised water activities.

10. Enrol your child in a good quality early childhood centre that has high teacher-to-child ratios and that values free play (emergent curriculum) and the outdoors

Ages 7 – 10

Physical connection to self

1. More advanced relay races with others and teams, encouraging friendly competition.

2. Obstacle courses which require multiple challenges such as standing on one leg and hopping while throwing etc.

3. Athletics at home, such as long jump and high jump.

4. Basketball, soccer, tag or rugby and other team sports.

5. Go home stay home with friends or siblings or ban them from inside for an hour and see what they come up with.

6. Bull rush (yes even though our schools banned it).

7. Wheelbarrow racing with or without a wheelbarrow.

8. Making huts and forts, playing house (clean up after is valuable too).

9. Handstand competition in and out of water, water fights

10. Skateboarding, scootering, roller blading and other balanced based movement activities with equipment.

Ages 11 – 14

Physical connection to their strength/purpose

1. Tug of war or anything which demonstrates their developing strength.

2. Headstands or long handstands, cartwheels or gymnastics.

3. Parkour, gymnastics, ninja warrior games etc.

4. Athletics or yoga, and you can exercise together.

5. Formal sports teams or dance groups, competition level if desired.

6. Incentive based exercise programmes such as a fun run or fundraising events.

7. Long bush hikes with a delicious picnic at the end.

8. Independent bike rides through streets or forest alone or with friends.

9. Hang out times with friends at the local basketball court, skate park, or forest.

10. Extended time in nature such as at the zoo, with trees, at the beach, in the waves and other aspects of nature that

remind them of their place in this world and the strength of nature.

Ages 15 – 18

Connection to their place and role in the world

By this stage your child is becoming a young adult and has their own interests, likes and dislikes. The key here is to extend their skill to a higher level. Allow for challenge, advanced team work and more advanced physical abilities.

1. Extreme sports/activities such as bungy jumping.

2. High paced water sports, kayaking, paddle boarding.

3. Regular runs/walks together or with friends.

4. Skiing/snowboarding.

5. Sophisticated skate parks.

6. Family Frisbee competitions.

7. Extended family sports tournaments/camps.

8. Coming of age overnight bush trip.

9. More difficult hikes and tramps such as at national parks, or for full days

10. Competition level dance crews and troupes

11. Swimming championships

12. Bi-lateral integration exercises (fine tuning the movement on both sides of the body to work efficiently).

13. Manual dexterity games such as picking up marbles with your toes, or using each finger independently.

Even though they will always be your baby, at this age, they aren't a child any more. The consistent effort you have put in should now be showing benefits and they will begin to take ownership over their health and exercise. There is a transition from us providing opportunity and direction for our children to them choosing for themselves. Hopefully they will have a degree of internal acceptance and understanding of the reasons why this is important, and how it will benefit them. If we have been explaining this 'why' in their earlier years, and discussing what they get out of being active, they should now be in a place where this is 'normal' for them. In saying that, teens are teens! And you will always have periods of time where their bed is more alluring than exercise.

Keep encouraging and providing good nutrition through these teen years and make sure family outings are fun and engaging. Again, the best way to encourage the right behaviour is to do it ourselves! Go ahead and put yourself first for a while and take care of your own health. You deserve it. And it will show your children that this is a positive way to live.

Constandi (2016) reminds us that 'while the human brain reaches its full size by about 16 years of age, the prefrontal cortex does not reach full maturity until pruning is complete, and these gradual brain changes are associated with changes in behaviour. The frontal cortex is associated with complex functions such as decision making, action of rewards and, because it takes so long to reach full maturity, adolescents tend to place great emphasis on gaining approval from their peers, and often engage in risky behaviour to do so'.

Though our children may look like young adults, their brain is going through a tough time. Throughout life the brain continues to create new synapses and to eliminate unused ones, and both of these processes play important roles in learning, memory and other aspects of normal brain function. As we are patient and encouraging with them, they will also learn to be the same. Life is a journey, not a destination. Enjoy the ride and take your children with you; you will never look back.

Action Points

What was your biggest 'Ah-ha!' moment of this section on the vestibular system and movement?

What are you immediately going to apply, change, or do now that you know this information?

Top Three Points to Ponder

- All movement is beneficial for your child because it trains the vestibular system and other physical systems. This vestibular system is foundational for all learning, development, emotional regulation, and academics.

- Specific movement can train and retrain the brain, giving better academic achievement, emotional control, and physical coordination.

- Aim for holistic development, the mind, body, emotions and spirit. Movement accomplishes all of this. #thenaturalchildhoodmovement

'The purpose of life, after all, is to taste experience to the utmost, to reach out eagerly and without fear for newer and richer experience'.

~ **Eleanor Roosevelt**

L·O·V·E

Exploration

E

Exploration

Exploration, n. the action of travelling in or through an unfamiliar area in order to learn about it

> *Exploration encourages imagination, critical thinking, creativity, and wonder. It leads to a love of learning and the notion that one can dream. We then offer our dreams back to the world in the way of inventions, theories, creative works, service, contributions and altruism.*

Do you remember your favourite playtime activity as a child? Was it 'cops and robbers' at dusk, with your best mates screaming around the back yard? Or was it a birthday sleepover, where you talked until the early hours of the morning, eating junk food and being hushed by your parents? When we sit and imagine what it was that created a love for life, a curiosity for learning and satisfaction in a day as a child, it usually comes down to when we were discovering something new. Being curious and having our curiosity satisfied.

Often at times, when we remember back, it was a sensory experience lived to the full. Running through whipping grass as the wind wraps around you. Eating cold ice cream on a hot day with it dripping down your fingers and making your hands sticky. Hearing words of affirmation from a close friend. Our bodies love to learn and in learning we love. We were once those starry-eyed children with an uncomplicated love and thirst for life. Our children are too.

When we look at children and their thirst for life the above definition resonates loudly. From the moment they are born they reach out, peer curiously at the world around them, and have hearts wide open. They are not fearful of failing, of others, or of anything. They come into the world loving it and wanting more, exploring, intrigued and curious. This spark of life is a gift and one that must be nurtured in our children.

Einstein said, 'the one thing that is more powerful than knowledge is imagination'. This is a powerful sentiment in an age of information overload. Rather than focusing on filling our children with knowledge that everyone else has, we need to balance that with 'white space', or free-thinking time for their imaginations to run free.

Today, the speed at which information travels, the depth of knowledge found, and the scientific research discovered every week is astonishing. We are the most connected, and therefore potentially most intelligent generation in human history. Our resources far outnumber what civilisations had in years past. Even though information is at our fingertips and constantly and readily evolving, we seem as a society to be growing simpler, more foolish, even. We repeat history, making the same mistakes. Do we use the information we have to build knowledge that contributes to this earth? The evidence is in our actions.

'Rather than focusing on filling our children with knowledge that everyone else has, we need to balance that with 'white space', or free-thinking time for their imaginations to run free'.

The principle of exploration is to create a space for your child's own creativity, choices, and contribution to the world. After imparting and investing all our thoughts, values, and principles to our children, the principle of exploration allows them to wonder, develop and expand their interests and abilities; to become geniuses in their own way and sphere.

When a child is curious, awed and wondering about something, new neural pathways are being formed in their brain. Wonder and curiosity are essential for learning, loving life and forming understanding. Imagine what life would be like without exploration. A mere continuance of mediocre routine. The same old, day after day. There would be no discoveries no new countries found. No new knowledge, no inventions, no art. Never pushing the boundaries of our physical world, or selves. Just the same thing every day, week, and year for generations.

Imagination brings out and develops the spirit of your child. When they imagine they dream; they release their inner self. Exploring new things is essential to feeling fulfilled in life, in feeling whole and satisfied. As humans we have a natural inclination to discover, develop, seek and explore. We want to know more; to understand what is out there. Without this drive we wouldn't envision architecture that pushes physical boundaries, we would never have built hospitals or social services that seek to better mankind. We are made to think outside of the box and explore what else there is, what else can be done, and how we can do it. Our children are no different.

From the moment a child is born they innately want to move and explore and look at what is around them. Maybe you have experienced the amazement in a newborn's eyes as they first look at you. Or had that two-year-old who will not stop touching everything! It's in us from birth, but unfortunately many of us have it stripped out of us.

Do you remember the first time you were overtaken by that sense of awe and wonder?

Maybe it was the first books you read? When you became engrossed in the characters and their story that you just had to read it over and over again? Maybe it was the rhyming words and flow of the voice that drew you in, or that it lulled you to sleep that made you desperate to read it every day. Or as an adult, that book you just couldn't put down so you did silly things like staying up until 2am just to finish it, knowing you would pay for it the next day. That is wonder, awe and curiosity.

'When we give our children opportunities to experience feelings of gratitude and pride, it creates self-determination, an ability to drive themselves to achieve that which they desire'.

Or was it when you first heard a new instrument, how the sound plucked at your ears and drew your attention? How it created emotion and caused you to imagine, made you want to hear it again, dance along, or maybe learn to play it.

Or maybe you saw something magnificent, a building touching the heavens, or waterfalls cascading over rounded rocks, or a boat bigger than a hotel hovering on still waters. You stood awestruck as your mind absorbed what was in front of you taking in the moment. When you recall an experience like this you remember what wonder feels like. It is an overwhelming joy, excitement and amazement combining together to move you emotionally and cognitively. It creates a desire to achieve more, be more, to see, create, dance, draw or write. Often it draws out gratitude – and it's positively tremendous when we experience it.

When we give our children opportunities to experience gratitude and pride it creates self-determination, an ability to drive themselves to achieve that which they desire. They become the directors of their own lives and learning. They don't need parents who push, cajole, bribe or threaten them to learn something. They can motivate themselves to achieve the outcomes they want. The more we allow our children to experience wonder, the more they will love learning, whether formal or informal, and own the process themselves. It empowers them with joy. It feeds them. We just need to provide the resources, the experiences, and the opportunities they need to engage.

I currently have one child interested in drawing. He loves it. Whenever he has free time (without devices) he draws. He can spend hours sitting there drawing, showing everyone, beaming with pride at his creations—and he chooses it. When

I saw how much he had done—half a ream of paper and a couple of clear files full—I knew this was his passion. I made sure to encourage his efforts. Yep, I did need to give the 'don't criticise' talk to myself, because it's all too easy to tell him what is not right about the pictures. But having failed many times with that in the past I knew I needed to make wiser choices this time. I am stunned with how much he loves drawing when he feels he is doing well at it. He doesn't need me pointing out what is wrong with it, I am sure those thoughts go through his head without reinforcement from me. He just needs me to be amazed at what he can do—because he is amazed too. Watching him show his art to others and give his pictures away as presents encourages me that he has been sparked to explore the possibilities and potential of his abilities. Something he has that no one has ever tapped into before.

Explore Lifelong learning

As parents we can help to grow our children's sense of exploration by providing new opportunities to experience, and by having conversations surrounding their interests. Schools are starting to adopt this philosophy with the Inquiry Learning process which allows children to choose their topic of learning and create their own learning experiences with support. As parents, we don't need to wait for school to do this for our children, we can do it with the simplest things at home.

When my daughter was twelve years old, she was far too interested in Netflix. We discussed what she would like to do instead. I told her that she needed a hobby. In the beginning she was absolutely horrified. She didn't want to join a sport, learn an instrument or do anything that I thought was remotely beneficial. This discussion went on for days and once I enforced the time boundaries around Netflix, I could see she was becoming very bored so she began to think of something. (Note here: often it's easier for us if we simply change the environment rather than engage in endless arguments).

After a couple of days of this, she asked for a creative space and I agreed. It took less than an hour to sort and rearrange the back shed so that she could have her own space. She did most of the work in creating this space and I let her arrange it however she liked. She needed to empty all the items that were being stored in there and together we found new homes for them. She cleaned the benches, created a chair and desk out of bits and pieces, and organized all the art materials that we had. She had complete ownership. When she had finished, she had a usable, creative space with the resources to do what she could imagine.

This was an empowering process for my daughter, as she came up with the idea, had the motivation to do it, and accomplished it with little assistance from me. She saw herself as capable and really enjoyed the time she spent in there drawing, conceptualising ideas, asking for support, and carrying out projects. It wasn't an easy process though, for either of us. She had to stretch herself to come up with and do something that she wasn't used to, and I had to be patient while she couldn't make up her mind! And when she did make up her mind, all that was running through my head was 'I don't have time to do this right now!' But I gritted my teeth, put on my nice voice and helped her do it. And the rewards for making the effort were well worth it.

> **'Making a first step, whatever it might be, will start your process of change. It may be writing a plan, cleaning something out, having a discussion, changing a routine. Whatever it is, do it. It is liberating to create the change you are wanting, to explore new things and experiences that you haven't before.'**

It can be really hard to create something different in our children's lives as well as our own. We have the right ideas, listen to the right teaching and some of us are blessed enough to have the right support. But at the end of the day, it's still blimmin' hard. That is just the truth, and not much will change that. Apart from one day, just doing it. Just starting that thing you have been thinking about for your children. Making that first step, whatever it might be, will start your process of change. It may be writing a plan, cleaning something out, having a discussion, changing a routine.

Whatever it is, do it. It is liberating to create the change you are wanting, to explore new things and experiences that you haven't before. Actions can change feelings and empower you. Do the right thing and you will feel right. Just take one step at a time. We gain confidence by repeated success and that starts with the first action. It feels the same for our children as well. Why not make a start on that thing today? Just one thing. Five minutes. Then plan for tomorrow.

There are many practical ways to create an environment of exploration, and again, not one thing will suit everyone. Link it with your passions and interests and just do what works for you. There isn't an age barrier for exploration. I have read a story of a couple in their 70's going out camping and tramping in the wilderness for a week! Now that's exploration! I can only hope that I will be of the fittest health and wellness at 70 to do the same. Whether we are six months, six years, 26 or 60, exploration is an attitude and a state of mind.

Exploration is wanting to learn more, trying something new and getting involved. It is critically questioning what we do and what else can be done. This is what we are doing here. Go on, give yourself a pat on the back for making those changes.

The latest research is also showing that the people who live the longest and who are the happiest are those who are grateful for what they have. When we couple that with the attitude of lifelong learning—always seeking and curiously delving into life—we have a recipe for success. Being grateful for things in our lives is something that we need to learn through practice. Gratitude hasn't always been popular in society, but it is essential. We can actually feel happier if we choose to think about things that we are thankful for. It's a simple action with profound influence. Teaching and encouraging our children to do this also sets them up for positive mental health. You can do this together in the car in the morning, or before bed at night, or at the dinner table together. However you choose, adding gratitude into your daily life will positively benefit your whole family.

Are you wondering if there are other ways you can parent better? Wondering if there is something different you can do to raise happy, healthy children? Or wondering what mistakes

My daughter trying out photography and watercolours. This stemmed from the shed idea.

others have made and what learning you can adopt, not just in parenting, but in all of life? Then you are a lifelong learner. You have the attitude that there is always something new to learn. You accept that to change, you need to learn something new, and that learning can be fun. You are setting the example of learning for your children and that is amazing! Lifelong learning is what it sounds like. We adopt an attitude to learn thoughout life. There are no barriers except our own beliefs.

What follows is a range of ways we can practically implement the principle of exploration. They are a range of suggestions that you can fit into your own time, space and family culture. Take a look at the underlying principles and values in what is suggested here and implement them in a way that works for your individual family needs.

'Whether we are six months, six years, 26 or 60, exploration is an attitude and a state of mind.'

Too often we think that learning only happens at school and in homework time. However, I strongly believe we are our children's first teachers, and learning happens all day, every day. Say your four-year-old loves dinosaurs then do everything dinosaurs! Cakes, museum, toys (borrow or buy), make them with crafts, create their footprints in sand or plaster of Paris. Read stories, watch programmes, and do anything else you can do!

The more you saturate your children's minds with different knowledge about their topic of interest the more they will enjoy and learn. Keep adding to their depth of knowledge—you may be surprised just how much history and very long words a four-year-old can learn about dinosaurs! One of the boys at preschool knew the names of twenty dinosaurs! Have you ever heard a three-year-old pronounce 'Mamenchisaurus'?

Of course, this applies not only to dinosaurs, but whatever your child is interested in, whether it be birds; ballerinas; or like one of mine, snails. One of my boys was intently fascinated with snails when he was three, it was all he ever talked about and looked for. I was completely tired of snails, and the whole thing was all really sticky and yucky, but I just couldn't get him past it, so I embraced it instead. He had a birthday cake in the shape of a snail, and hilariously, a snail party. We raced snails on pieces of paper and even created art with them by watching them move over paper. He even learnt about caring for nature and his own strength by, you guessed it, squishing a few of them accidentally. (I hope nature can forgive me for the many snails sacrificed for his learning). It was crazy snail city at our place for months. But then it ended. Just like that, he was finished, he had learnt what he thought was important, he satisfied his curiosity, and now he no longer needed to do it. Literally, one day it was snails and the next day it was... volcanoes! (Yes, that was messy too!!)

Explore Self

The Mindfulness movement has been increasingly embraced by Western society and the positive results on people's sense of peace, attention, and happiness is evident. There are now programmes for children in schools to help them become more connected with their thoughts and find a sense of peace. This is not something I practise every day with my children as a discipline like meditation, but it is a tool to help them connect with what is going on inside their heads.

Metacognition is thinking about our thinking, and when we make the time to be still, children can become aware of the many things that go on in their minds. Awareness is the first step in understanding and changing any behaviour therefore it is key that our children learn to become aware of their inner thoughts and feelings. As a parent you can provide a quiet space and ask leading questions to help them explore their own thought processes and self talk. Even though the child is the only one who can recognize the thoughts inside their mind and decide to change them, we can support this process through love, patience, role modelling and quality questions.

Teens can be often quite moody (everyone with a teen say amen!), and they can easily flip through a hundred different emotions in an hour. Helping them become aware of their thoughts supports their understanding of their emotions. In the case of one of my teens, when he gets angry about something, he has learnt to go to the boxing bag to punch it out. This is a great way to get rid of all his pent-up energy from feeling angry and helps to release the rush of testosterone and adrenalin that occurs. But there are other times where sitting and thinking through the thoughts that caused the emotions and actions is just as helpful. Sometimes your child can process the thoughts that lead to emotions and actions by themselves and sometimes they need someone to ask precise questions to spur the thinking. By actively encouraging this process and supporting him through it he gains the awareness that leads to change. This is a much more effective strategy than telling them to get over it, or to stop the behaviour. It deals with the root of the behaviour instead.

Even in our parenting journey, being mindful and aware of our own thoughts, emotions and actions, and the links between them, will support us in our own growth in raising our children. When we recognise why we become annoyed at certain behaviour we can then change our thoughts, which will lead to a change in actions.

'Sometimes your child can process the thoughts that lead to emotions and actions by themselves, and sometimes they need someone to ask the precise questions to spur the thinking.'

DAD'S SAY

As a dad I have found that life is full of exploration—mostly of my own self. Who I am as a man, a son, a husband and a dad. One area that stands out the most in this is discipline. How do I discipline and why do I do it like that?

I realised that what I was doing when disciplining my children was not always best and I have had to explore other ways of doing it. It took me a while to come to the realisation that it was me who needed to change, that maybe there was a better way for my children, even if I hadn't been raised that way. Physical discipline was a big part of how I was raised, and I remember how it felt as a young child. I remember never getting an apology and sometimes not even knowing what I had done to deserve the discipline. I knew that I didn't want my children to have that same experience, so I had to relearn discipline.

I felt stupid to begin with and I've failed many times, but I have never given up learning. In this way, I show my kids what it takes to be a lifelong learner as a dad, to show them humility before I ask for it, and to respect them so they know how to respect me and others. I grow with my kids and explore our relationship together, always remaining open to learn new things.

I use this principle of exploring and understanding to get to know them better. The journey to understanding my kids hasn't been easy because it was different to anything I had known. In my world growing up, it wasn't the job of the parent to know and understand the child, it was the job of the child to obey their parents. I had to change that view and in becoming aware of it, I have been able to change, and my kids have benefitted too. Their normal is different to what mine was. I am still who I am. I haven't changed me. I have just changed the way I relate to them and I do this happily.

When thinking about exploration an area that boys in particular need to explore is risk. They need it to learn and grow. No ifs or maybes, it's a must! There is something hard wired in boys that craves adventure. Boys and girls need different things to grow the best they can. We have seen that first-hand with three boys and one girl. I have found that one thing my boys have appreciated the most is my realness and authenticity and times to have fun together. Boys need the chance to take some risks, even if mum isn't so happy about it, and I see how important it is for them to have this at a young age. They need a time and place where there aren't any rules, where they can have freedom, really go wild and be free.

As my children grow up, I see more and more the need to reach them where they are, and to stop trying to make them fit me. When I explore these new ways of parenting, I explore myself. I will continue to explore new learning, recognise who I am authentically, and change to be who I want to be with my kids. I hope in the future I look back and can say that I am still changing as a man. Still exploring new ways, and that my kids are doing it with me too.

Explore Critical Thinking

On an academic level we can also ask critical questions to explore thinking even if there is no specific answer. When they are encouraged to ask questions, our children are reasoning and forming their own opinions and thoughts. If you don't agree with their opinions, you can always ask another question that will help them re-evaluate their perspective.

For example, you can ask a four year old, 'Why do you think the sky is blue?' Maybe the answer will be 'Because there is water up there'. This would indicate the reference point for their previous experience of water and seeing it blue. Your reply could be something like, 'Maybe, that's interesting, and if there was water up there why isn't it falling down?' By having your child challenge their own and other people's thinking, no matter what age, they are learning that reasoning can be changed, and new possibilities can be created.

Critical thinking really is the backbone of success in the formal learning setting. If your child can understand the processes of critical thinking early on you are setting them up for success at school. Don't be afraid of questions that reflect a curious mind. Of course, it should go without saying that the tone and way we question will determine the response. If we question with a negative attitude, belittle them, or mock that they don't know something then they won't want to answer. But if we keep it light-hearted, curious and open, they will naturally respond. Kids love to talk about what they know when they feel like they can be the expert in something.

Teachers will be familiar with Bloom's Taxonomy (the process for developing higher thinking, or critical skills). Here is an image of what it looks like:

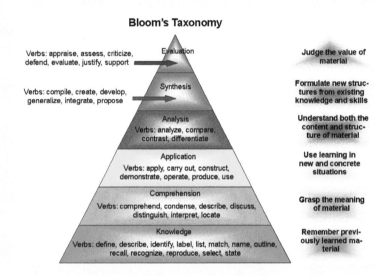

This method is used to develop higher level thinking in the classroom at any age. The children first start to know a new piece of information – a ball for example. 'My ball is round and light.' The comprehension or understanding stage is when they can discuss and describe that ball in more depth. 'It is orange and slightly fluffy, if I squeeze it, it moves, and my friend has one.' The application stage involves the use and application of the knowledge. 'I can throw the ball to my friend and we have fun together. I can use the ball to bounce and I can only hold two balls at one time. The ball can be used for different things.' The analysis stage is where they may compare and differentiate the knowledge. 'My ball is orange but my friend's is yellow and his is smaller than mine. His ball can go faster. If I throw my ball with my left hand it doesn't go as far as with my right.' The knowledge will then be synthesized to form a new rationale. 'My ball is made of plastic and it bounces because there is air inside of it. If it goes flat it will not bounce, usually the smaller ball bounces higher than the bigger ball.' Finally, the last stage is evaluating the knowledge 'My friend's ball is better than mine because it's faster, at play time I will make sure that I get his ball first so that I can use it because I can throw it the fastest. Smaller balls are better than bigger balls.'

This is a simplified version of a thought process that could occur in seconds. However, the end product is critical thinking about the subject. Making a judgement on the information as useful or not, and how to use it in personal application. I would encourage every teacher to reflect on the content of their lessons and ensure there is time for children to develop their thinking through these stages. Ask leading questions and organise activities that will help them examine and explore their thinking more.

Explore a Growth Mindset

A growth mindset for children is absolutely essential to their success through school, life and in their future careers. This makes it another important area for exploration. The work of Dwek (2006) on the ability to be flexible, adaptable and positive in our thoughts has changed the way we look at education. If you need more information on this there is a list of books in the Further Reading section. Essentially it is the ability to recognise our thoughts and understand which ones are helping or hindering us. The ability to choose positive thoughts and words will determine our children's lives!

An example may be that a child goes from 'I suck at maths' to 'I am learning how to do math'. The shift may seem minor but in motivational and psychological terms it is huge. If you suck at something you aren't going to try to do it, are you? If you repeat these sorts of messages, you convince your brain that they're true. So if you decide that nothing is going to get better no matter what you do, then that is exactly what you will get! Our words and thoughts become self-fulfilling prophecies due to the way our brains process information.

A well-used quote from Henry Ford is, 'Whether you think you can, or you think you can't, you are probably right'. By teaching our children that their thoughts really determine their destiny they become empowered to take hold of the course of their lives instead of leaving it to chance. As adults we can recognise that most of our success in life is due to our perspective of experiences. If we think things are hard and bad and life is always like that, then that is exactly what life becomes, because that is the only option we can see. But if we see things as learning experiences, as opportunities to grow and change and develop, while still recognising that they are difficult, then we will become a lifelong learner. Exploring these different philosophies and practices releases us from the boring mundane routine of life. We find and discover ways that we can get what we expect and that makes life a party! An adventure just waiting to happen. That is why acknowledging that we are all learning and growing and identifying the areas of strength and weakness within ourselves, provides us with the ability to keep growing.

> **'If we see things as learning experiences, as opportunities to grow and change and develop ... then we will become a lifelong learner'.**

Some ways that we can encourage our children to have a growth mindset is by talking and working through times when they have 'failed'. I say 'failed' for lack of a better term, because a growth mindset acknowledges that there really is no failure, just lessons to learn. Discussing children's thoughts about it and helping them see a different way of looking at things empowers them. Even through everyday interaction, we can encourage a growth mindset. When kids make mistakes at home, or cause accidents— even the typical spilt milk example—we can help them move on and through it positively. Instead of yelling about why they spilt the milk (because really, they don't know) we can ask them what they need to do now, and what they could do better next time (this demonstrates our own growth mindset too!).

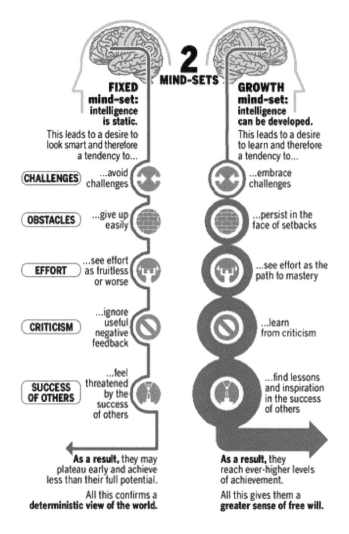

Sourced from embracingpossibility.com

Dr Caroline Leaf is another leader in the field of our minds and thoughts and their impact on our success in life. Her works are also referenced in the section at the back of this book. Essentially Leaf's research agrees with and adds to Dwek's works by then giving practical tools to identify our thoughts and a proven way to change them. Her research has shown that this leads to physical structural changes in the brain. The ability we have to control our thoughts, emotions and brain is astounding. We must realise that each and every conversation and learning experience imprints itself on our children's brains. If we can get our children learning and understanding a growth mindset early in life, we are setting them up for success in whatever they do. I highly recommend you go and read some of Dr Leaf's books because it will absolutely change the way you think about our choice of influence over our brains!

> **'We must realise that each and every conversation and learning experience imprints itself on our children's brains.'**

Explore Grit

Yet another powerful trait to explore and develop in our children is grit. The art of just never giving up. Plain, good old-fashioned persistence. The book entitled Grit by Angela Duckworth (2016), discusses the research that has been undertaken on some of the most successful people or top achievers in the world. The common thread between all of these people is that they all have the trait of grit. She explains how grit is a combination of both power and passion which produces an attitude of never giving up.

Applying this knowledge to our parenting is a constant struggle. At times we need to allow our kids the freedom to find for themselves what they can do, and at other times we may need to help them to achieve what they are wanting. Still at other times we need to push a bit harder to help them learn that they can do it, even when they think they can't. Then at other times, we allow them to experience the joy and pain of pushing through alone. It is good for our children to feel the excitement of having something they want to achieve and allowing them the struggle to achieve it, so that they begin to know exactly what they are capable of. We also have the privilege of learning and pushing our own boundaries, developing our own sense of grit and being the role model our children need.

Would anyone agree with me that modern society is often overly concerned with cotton-wooling our children? We are intent on making them safe, healthy and well, and these urges are common. But to never be hurt physically or emotionally, to always be okay and never in pain is an unrealistic view of child development. We have difficult times as adults so it is best to support our children to handle these kinds of times while they are young, to help equip them for adulthood. Life is a process of learning lessons and the brain learns best through either pain or pleasure. The unfortunate truth is that our children need pain to learn lessons in life and if we take that opportunity away from them, we are doing them a disservice. As humans we learn from our experience. I am certainly not suggesting we purposely go out of our way to hurt them, but I am saying, let life teach them to a certain degree. And this is done in increasing degrees as they age.

The natural world, friendships, wrong choices, late assignments, bad timing and more will all cause pain, and help teach our children what they should or shouldn't do. Let's utilise the natural process to help them make more informed choices and to learn, instead of us just telling them. It is beneficial for our children to learn to push themselves at the times they need to. To persevere through hard or difficult situations and to determine to succeed. In fact, learning through natural consequences is the best form of discipline.

Some situations can be as simple as going to the doctor. A couple of my children really do not like blood tests. When the doctor orders one, I have hours, if not days, of tears, outbursts and fear. One time, they couldn't do the blood test until a couple of days later and my daughter was not happy. The whole time I never stopped hearing about how she didn't want to do it. She tried everything. Anger, tears, cuddles, pleading, puppy eyes and the like. After much discussion and convincing I stood my ground and told her it must be done. We cuddled, talked her through her fears, rationalised and eventually ignored. I had done all I could to support her through it, but in the end, she just needed to battle her thoughts herself. Right up to the moment that we were in the waiting room, she battled. We went in, she endured it reluctantly, then looked at me and smiled. In that moment she understood all that I was saying. It really was bigger in her mind than it was in reality, and it wasn't that bad after all. It is times like this that we need to stand beside our kids. Let them face their fear and let them have the satisfaction of overcoming it. Determination and persistence cannot be underrated. They are key character traits our children need for their future.

The teaching strategy of scaffolding is beneficial for reluctant learners. It is taking a child from where they are, and what they can do, and providing learning that is just outside their comfortable limits. This way it is like a ladder. One step at a time, they gain new and deeper understanding. We simply provide the stairs or scaffolds, for the children to climb and encourage them along, being their best cheerleader.

This teaching strategy embraces the process of learning rather than the potential of failure. It is essential that what we are providing for the children is not too easy or too hard. If things are too easy, then the child doesn't grow in learning or understanding. If they are too hard, they will lose motivation, feel incompetent and give up. Scaffolding is using what they know to take them one step further at the opportune time. It is important, therefore, to know where a child's level of understanding and development is so we can help them take that one extra step.

Explore Physicality

You have heard me say it before, but I will say it again: let your children explore the limits of their physical ability. Often, they have a limited view of what they can and can't do, and often we unconsciously encourage them to play small. When they want to climb to the top of the rope course, let them. If they want to jump off objects or zoom downhill on a bike, let them. Of course, I mean within reason, but often we can tend to be overly protective, or worry (out of love), much to their detriment.

As they explore their physical capabilities, they will learn how much they can and can't do, and those scraped knees, and maybe the odd broken bone at a young age will give them the knowledge of how much risk they should take when they are older. Pain is an effective teacher and a little now is better than a lot later. I would rather a broken arm from a skateboard at age six than a broken body from a car accident at sixteen. Wouldn't you? In addition to this, the child's brain gets all that amazing stimulation which was discussed under our "V" section.

'Pain is an effective teacher and a little now is better than a lot later.'

There is no age limit to challenging ourselves physically. From birth to age 100 there is always something we can do to improve our balance, movement, flexibility or strength. Often the only thing holding us back is our beliefs. 'I'm too old, too tired, not good enough, not fit enough, too sore, I can't'. If we believe these things we will be these things. If we allow our children to believe and say things just like this, then this is what they will be. Our bodies are amazing machines and there isn't much they can't do if they just try and practice.

I remember being in preschool with a class of 2-5-year-olds. I started to stretch my legs and back in different ways and soon enough there was a small group of children around me doing the same. We were laughing and playing with each other, seeing who could challenge who to do the next move. We ended up with 2-and-a-half-year-olds doing handstands

My son exploring what his body can do and learning to take measured risks.

against a wall and seeing who could hold it the longest. What an amazing learning experience initiated by the children themselves! Watching them display a can-do attitude and then practising until they mastered it. There is an intrinsic drive in all children to see how far, how fast, how good and how strong they can be. Use this to their own advantage.

Explore Creativity

Help your children explore the arts. It's easy to have preschoolers who go to kindergarten and paint and draw and build and craft, but it's not always easy to allow that mess at home. By allowing your child even the simplest of arts and crafts at home (even just paper and felts), your child can experiment with making a physical representation of their own thoughts.

Art challenges fine motor skills (holding a pencil, forming a shape, hand-eye coordination), as well as their perception qualities (accurate representation, reference points, and observance of detail). Who would have thought that so much learning can be done by doodling? Even if their creation may one day end up in the bin, it is the process of creating that develops their skills and abilities and an appreciation of beautiful things, rather than the end product. Therefore, don't worry too much about the perfection of their creation but encourage them to do what they can. Ask questions, notice their thinking. They may never become an artist but they can access a world of learning through art.

You can offer advice and knowledge and develop their understanding, but always season their creativity with encouragement. If the child feels like they cannot do anything properly, they will give up and this is not producing a love of learning or an attitude of exploration. No matter what age your children are you will be surprised how sophisticated their drawings can become when they are given freedom and encouragement with all the arts.

Creativity comes largely from experience and this starts from a very young age. What natural and sensory experiences are we giving our babies and toddlers? I encourage you to allow them to explore the outside environment; bugs, mud, beaches, and forests. These different textures, smells and sights build a library of information they will draw on throughout life. Even allowing them to mix many different kinds of experiences together - mud on paper, or spaghetti with Milo (yes, true story!) or whatever weird thing they decide is all learning. Again, it's not the product that is important but the learning process. Don't be afraid of the mess—it can be cleaned, and the learning will be worth it! Maybe your child might gravitate to that same flower for the tenth time and you are exasperated. Think of it as an opportunity to help them grow their wonder by doing something different with it. Draw it, eat it, plant it, gift it, and read about it...you get the idea.

There are many different art forms you can introduce your children to. The obvious ones are painting, colouring and drawing, but as they get older there are different forms of painting they can try – watercolours, sprays, oils. There is photography and sculpture. There are paper crafts, sewing, modelling, and the list goes on. If something sparks an interest in you then it may just do the same for your child. I encourage you to give it a go.

Exploring Empathy

It's important to let your children explore empathy. Empathy is the ability to feel or understand what another person is experiencing from their viewpoint. Through empathy we are always learning about ourselves and others as humans. It is a topic of endless interest which introduces practical skills and abilities. Through intentional guiding we can allow our children to explore a range of emotions, including some of the not-nice ones. This should be explored as you gauge their emotional maturity so that your child isn't shocked or traumatised (you will know your child).

Exploring difficult issues such as death, pain, or suffering can help a child in their exploration of emotions and understanding their role here on Earth. Depending on the child's age, we need to allow them to see and experience the feelings of other people who are suffering, whether from homelessness, sickness, famine or war. These can all serve to develop empathy.

The development of empathy and altruism (doing something for someone without expecting a reward) sets the human race apart from all other species. We have the gift to feel another person's pain and then offer some form of support. We also have an opportunity to help our children do the same. When we do this, we develop a beautiful, community-minded, caring character in our children. It changes who they are and how they see the world, and that is something to be proud of. It also develops the holistic child that we have been discussing. One who isn't just intellectually savvy but also has the emotional intelligence to support others. Feeling empathy for others and having the opportunity to act on it is just as important as passing their schooling.

'We have the gift to feel another person's pain and then offer some form of support. We also have an opportunity to help our children do the same.'

Children are very impressionable especially in their earlier years. When we allow them to experience emotional pain we help them understand how other people feel and can impress upon them the importance of caring for others. Community is about being there for others, helping, supporting, and empathising, joining with them through life and allowing others to join with us. When you allow your child that experience throughout their childhood you will develop a foundation of love for life. When we are wanting to teach lessons that our children will remember for their lifetime we need to incorporate both information and emotion. Information and emotion form a long-term memory. Painful times or feeling the pain of others, can also produce good memories, and the greatest teaching opportunities.

If you think maybe your children are too young to be exposed to this kind of pain, you can always get them a pet. I remember when we bought our seven-year-old son a guinea pig for his birthday. (This is the same fun loving, snail crazy, animal-mad child). He loved that pet. For a young child, he really doted upon it. He fed it, cleaned it, petted it, was bitten by it, and ran home to it after school each day. The day it died was one of the most painful times in his life. Innocent tears filled his eyes day after day as he processed his loss.

As a mum it is horrible to see your child upset, and you want to take their pain away, but the lesson that came from it was valuable. He learnt how to deal with pain and grief in a healthy way. He learnt that life is short. He learnt how to receive comfort and give comfort. He learnt to love big despite getting hurt. And he learnt about life and death. Years later when we had other guinea pigs that also died, the pain didn't feel as bad, and this time he could support his younger brother as he went through the same thing. He could comfort, support, empathise and give back. He had learnt that loving is the greatest gift and it's worth the temporary pain of loss just to experience it.

Let's not underestimate the power of connection to others. It is key to living. Experts are now finding that people who live the longest do so because of strong, healthy, loving relationships (along with good quality food and exercise). Developing strong connections with others is something that has to be taught, demonstrated, modelled and experienced in our digital age.

Maybe pets aren't for you. If you don't have them, or you don't like them, why not try some of these practical ideas (or find something that fits you better)? Keep in mind the age of your child and what will be appropriate for them.

- Explore homelessness and how that feels for others by serving at a homeless shelter.

- Adopt a sponsor child as a family and write often, learning and discussing what life is like for other people in the world. This also leads into gratitude which is essential for understanding empathy.

- You and your children can explore kindness towards animals by volunteering at the SPCA (animal shelter).

- Volunteer with other charitable organisations who need extra help.

- You can cook for neighbours or families who have just had babies, or friends who are out of work, all the while talking about the reasons why you are doing this, to help others because you can understand how it would feel to be in their shoes.

- In fact, you can just cook or bake for others just because it is a kind thing to do.

- You could even help your children save up pocket money or fundraise to make donations to a cause you believe in.

The opportunity to help others is endless and it is true that our greatest satisfaction in life comes from supporting others, contributing to their lives, and understanding our own value in this. Why not give this gift to your children?

'Children are very impressionable especially in their earlier years. When we allow them to experience emotional pain we help them understand how other people feel and can impress upon them the importance of caring for others.'

Here are my two eldest 'free-range' kids about seven years ago putting up a tent next to our free-range guinea pigs. They used to run free in the back yard! To put it in context we live in New Zealand's largest city—not on a rural farm.

Whatever you decide to do, ensure you take your child along for the journey and talk about it—a lot. Put words to the feelings and put actions to thoughts and explore the possibilities of empathy through care and service. Explain to your children why we spend time and money to invest in others, and in that they will develop gratitude for what has been given to them, as well as a heart centred on others.

Explore the Earth

We live in a time where the impact we as humans are having upon this earth has become so evident that we can no longer ignore it. We are aware of the consequences of our actions upon this planet and are living to see them. Recently, Australia had a heat wave, flash flooding and out of control fires, while northern America and Canada lost people to the coldest temperatures in decades. The decisions we have made as a human race will now have consequences not only for us but for our children. We are living with the effects of the industrial age, and how we live now will affect our children's future sooner than we hoped. When we educate our children about the earth, we are teaching them about their future selves.

I am excited to see how schools are confronting this problem and challenging our children on how to solve it. As parents we both lead and support this work by the way we personally live on the earth and teach our children how to steward and care for it. The easiest way to do this is through normal everyday life situations. Discuss rubbish and recycling and if possible, take a trip to the local rubbish dump. Talk about biodegradable and non-biodegradable products, clean up local parks, beaches and rivers, and involve your kids in choosing eco-friendly products. Of course, composting, or worm farming is a valuable learning exercise as well as being essential for the environment. Be sure to make the learning fun and engaging, but also relevant. We need to make this way of life normal and quickly, otherwise we will not have the planet we have for much longer.

Even a trip to the supermarket can create a whole new level of understanding for our children about the impact of our lifestyles on our planet. In many Western countries we can also attend workshops and practical lessons for free. I implore you to make every effort to connect your child to the world, and to teach them how to care for, nurture and value it. That way not only will our children live peaceful, safe lives but so will our grandchildren and great grandchildren.

We need to educate our children about the consequences of everyday actions. Where does that cheap plastic toy come from? How much of the earth's resources did it take to make it? How valuable is it to you? Where will it go when it breaks or when you don't want it anymore? What is the actual cost to us and to the planet? Is it worth buying it? What else can we choose instead that will have better outcomes? Unless we are talking about these things our children will probably not think of them or learn the impact of our choices on the planet.

The kitchen can be one of the best learning environments for this. Think of everything you use in your kitchen in just one day. The food, the wrappings, the cleaning products, the drinks. Think of how many of these things can be reused, recycled or swapped out for an environmentally friendly alternative. Why not discuss this with your older children and come up with ideas together on how you can reduce waste? Often you may just find that this will also save you money – so it's a win-win.

Another pertinent kitchen hack is the concept of head to tail, or zero wastage of food. We need to think how we can use all of the product. Such as all of the animal – if you eat meat. Utilizing bones for stock, or carcasses for soups. Or if, for example, you make a delicious home made apple pie, you can save and dry the peelings of the apples for teas; you can compost the core for your garden. Make the pastry by hand so you reduce that packaging, and throughout all of this, you are teaching your children the principles of not wasting. This is bound to save you money too.

There is a push now in our schools and communities to ensure we are working to protect our environment. This is a great start, but I firmly believe that more needs to be done and quickly. However, this doesn't mean it can't be fun! Challenge your children with creative tasks: how to use a bottle or lid again; what to make out of a cereal box; how to decorate their room; making homemade beeswax wraps to replace plastic wrap, making bags for groceries; saving jars for bulk bins; choosing paper over plastic...the list goes on and on. Enjoy this time together while knowing that you are setting up the future actions and beliefs of your child and their future family. This is a powerful difference we can make in their lives and in the world.

'The decisions we have made as the human race will now have consequences not only for us but also for our children'.

Action Points

What was your biggest 'ah-ha!' moment of this section?

What change are you immediately going to make?

Top Three Points to Ponder

◎)) Looking at our world curiously and in wonder helps us to explore all aspects of life, and helps our children to develop a positive mindset. This will set them up for success in their future as a lifelong learner.

◎)) Develop a spirit of generosity in your child by exploring the earth, their community, and ways that they can contribute to others' lives.

◎)) Explore different ways of thinking and knowing; beliefs determine thoughts, thoughts determine emotions, and emotions drive actions. Our actions either support or hinder our success.

'It is the supreme art of the teacher to awaken joy in creative expression and knowledge'.

~ **Albert Einstein**

Bits at the back of the book

Afterword

I hope this book has inspired you. I hope that sharing my thoughts and experiences has encouraged you to feel that you can, right now, make positive changes in your family life. I hope that hearing about some of my failings helped show you that we are all on the same path of parenthood, and I hope that the research behind these principles gives you assurance that they are beneficial.

I've arranged these key concepts into an acronym so that you can easily remember it wherever you go. I've tried to provide practical applications so that you can continue your journey of parenthood with a clear, positive road before you. I encourage you to remember to speak and express the languages of love to your child, allow a strong attachment to form and develop that into the formal processes of language. Continue to develop and stretch your child's language capabilities throughout their years by using positive and purposeful words. Combine this with purposeful listening as you allow them to share their heart.

I also hope you can enjoy the outdoors together, establishing and building strong relationships and powerful bodies in the context of your place in your community and our world. Take small daily moments to connect to all that is around you and allow it to bring you peace, and pass that peace onto your children. Take some risks outdoors and try something new. Explore a new side of yourself and your children that you may never have known before.

Above all, allow your children to move, encourage them to move and give them ample opportunities to do so. This will benefit every area of their lives. They will be happier, fitter, healthier, stronger, more connected and more intelligent. Move with them, enjoy it, laugh about it and just give it a go. From birth until the day they leave home, make movement, exercise, and physical health a normal and fun part of your family.

Explore. Explore all that is around you. Explore what you don't know. Explore new possibilities and opportunities. Believe in all that is good and possible in the world and encourage your children to do the same. Push the boundaries of limiting thoughts and beliefs, and establish in your children the mind, heart and passion to be, go, do, learn and create.

My final encouragement to you is to keep going. Don't give up. Don't give in to 'It's too hard'. Allow yourself to be supported as you also in turn, support others. Be kind to yourself—you don't know everything, and you don't have to. You just need to know that you are making a difference in your child's life. Let me say that again.

You. Are. Making. A. Difference.

In fact, THE defining difference.

Just by raising your children the best you can, and learning along the way, you are changing the future of our world. You are raising leaders. You are fulfilling a great purpose in this life. You are meaningful. This work is meaningful. You can do it. Be brave. Join the Natural Childhood Movement. Take your place.

Love. Love them. Just love them. Speak. Attach. Appreciate. Move. Explore. Learn. Love.

From my family to yours, may your family grow closer each day as we learn how to L.O.V.E. our children.

Leanne

Acknowledgements

I thank my children for essentially letting me 'test and try' nearly every form of parenting and schooling there is! Your unconditional love and growth has spurred me on to be the best mother I can be. Thank you for teaching me.

To my husband Joe, who continually demonstrates the humility to grow and change. We would not be who we are today without you. You are invaluable to our children.

I thank my mum Mary from whom I received my love of nature and passion for thrifty cooking. If it wasn't for you, I wouldn't be here. We live. We learn. We grow. Thank you for doing all you can. I also acknowledge my fathers John and Warren who have provided for, and guided me, and helped shape who I am today.

A special thanks to everyone who has supported, sharpened and encouraged me over the years. My success is your success.

Stock Photos, Photography and illustrations from:

Burst

Brgfx

Freepik

Ken Buist

Pexels

Sylvia Duckworth

Unsplash

Grit Becker

Cover: Kretchmar Design

Design Support: Yvonne Godfrey

Resources, Rhymes And Games

The following pages contain action rhymes that are common in early childhood settings and new entrant classes. They are great for young children as they incorporate song and rhyme into their learning, which engages and motivates them.

Songs and rhymes teach your child to develop an awareness of different emotions by allowing them to explore their own. They also support speech development because of the repetition of words. It develops hand-eye coordination by getting a good sense of beat from music, and improves memory skills by singing favourite songs regularly. Your child will begin to understand concepts such as night, day, under, over, animals and weather, which are the beginnings of mathematics and science. It develops timing skills which help them with coordination, as well as gross motor and fine motor skills and manual dexterity.

Use these to have some fun and build your relationship with your child – knowing that you are also building their brains.

(There are many more available on the internet too, so do a search and find ones that work for you).

Where is Thumbkin?

Where is Thumbkin?
Where is Thumbkin?
Here I am!
Here I am!
How are you today, Sir?
Very well. I thank you!
Run away! (Hide your hand behind your back)
Run and hide! (Hide your hand behind your back)

Start this rhyme with both hands behind your back with fists closed. Use your thumbs when you first begin, as if they are people talking to each other.

Then carry on with the next finger:
Where is Pointer?
Repeat the rhyme.
Then use Tall Man
Then Ring Man
Then Pinky or Baby

Here is the Beehive

Here is the beehive
(make a fist)
Where are the bees?
Hiding inside where nobody sees
Watch them come creeping out of the hive
One, two, three, four, five
(release one finger at a time from the fist/hive)
...BUZZ-ZZZ
(wiggle fingers)

Five Green, Speckled Frogs

Five green and speckled frogs
(hold up five fingers)
Sat on a speckled log,
Eating the most delicious bugs,
Yum, yum!
(rub tummy with other hand)
One jumped into the pool
(tuck one finger down)
Where it was nice and cool,
Then there were four green speckled frogs,
Glub, glub!

Four green and speckled frogs...
(Continue until there are no more speckled frogs on the log).

Wind Your Bobbin Up

Wind your bobbin up, wind your bobbin up,
Pull, pull, clap! clap! clap!
Wind your bobbin up, wind your bobbin up,
Pull, pull, clap! clap! clap!

Point to the ceiling, point to the floor,
Point to the window, point to the door.
[Repeat chorus]

Point to your fingers, point to your toes,
Point to your eyes and point to your nose.
[Repeat chorus]

Incy, Wincy Spider

Incy, Wincy Spider
Climbed up the waterspout
Down came the rain
And washed poor Incy out.
Out came the sun
And dried up all the rain
And Incy, Wincy spider
Went up the spout again.

Use your hand to be the spider that climbs up your child's body, tummy, or arm. Your child might like to be the spider and use their fingers to climb up your arm.

Head, Shoulders, Knees and Toes

Head, shoulders, knees and toes, knees and toes.
Head, shoulders, knees and toes, knees and toes.
And eyes and ears and mouth and nose
Head, shoulders, knees and toes, knees and toes.

When you are singing this song, show your child how to touch each part of the body that you are naming. You will need to start slowly at first, but as they get more confident you can build it up faster.

You can even try singing this using different body parts e.g. tummy, hips and thighs and fingers. This really helps children learn the names for the parts of their body.

Do Your Ears Hang Low?

Do your ears hang low? (Circle hands down from each ear)
Do they wobble to and fro? (Sway hands from side to side)
Can you tie them in a knot? (Make knot-tying actions)
Can you tie them in a bow? (Make bow-tying actions)
Can you toss them over your shoulder (Toss them over one shoulder)
Like a regimental soldier? (Salute/march)
Do your ears hang low?
(Repeat)

The Wheels on the Bus

The wheels on the bus go round and round,
(Roll forearms over one another in front of the body)
Round and round; round and round.
The wheels on the bus go round and round,
All day long.

The horn on the bus goes beep, beep, beep,
(Tap on your nose)
Beep, beep, beep; beep, beep, beep.
The horn on the bus goes beep, beep, beep,
All day long.

The lights on the bus go blink, blink, blink,
(Open and shut hands)
Blink, blink, blink; blink, blink, blink.
The lights on the bus go blink, blink, blink
All day long.

The wipers on the bus go swish, swish, swish,
(Make arms like windscreen wipers)
Swish, swish, swish; swish, swish, swish.
The wipers on the bus go swish, swish, swish,
All day long.

The driver on the bus says, "Move down the back."
(Make a hitchhiker's thumb and gesture behind you)
"Move down the back," "Move down the back,"
The driver on the bus says "Move on back," all day long.

I hope you enjoyed the finger rhymes! Now here are some easy movement activities that you children can do almost anywhere. These little games train the brain through the movement of the body. They develop balance, coordination, bilateral integration, fine and gross motor skills, and use movement and emotion to train memory.

They are short practical ways to put into practice all we have been reading about in these chapters.

Enjoy!

1. One Leg Balancing

Encourage your kids to try balancing on one leg while standing. See if you can get up to 10 seconds on each leg! If this is super easy for them try standing on a pillow on one leg. Or for more challenge get them to walk in a line, taking time in between each step. The change in surface will help to challenge their ability to balance. You can even try timing your kids to see who can balance the longest – they might just beat you!

This simple game develops the vestibular system which supports and controls balance. Physical balance is the key common ingredient in all learning in fact all learning relies on balance. Our bodies need it to sit and stand still. Our eyes need it to track across a page, our brains need it to be able to process information. Without a deep sense of balance we cannot focus properly.

2. Bedsheet Parachute

Parachutes are used a lot in pre-schools and you can quickly make a DIY parachute using a bedsheet. So, grab any size that you have – smaller can be more fun and challenging.

Get the kids (and you can join in!) to hold onto the end of the bedsheet and work together to try and shake a small stuffed animal or ball off of the parachute! You can add music and make rhythm. You can work large muscles by making large up and down movements. You can all lift it up and try to tuck it in around you so you make a cave inside.

This game develops gross motor skills and can help work on hand-eye coordination, spatial awareness, rhythm, communication, and relationships. All while they have fun!

3. Balloon Waddling Races

For this activity, you just need one balloon. To play, simply hold the balloon between your knees and waddle from one point to another without dropping the balloon. Waddle just like a penguin!

You could blow up multiple balloons if you'd like to have your kids' race against each other at the same time. However, you can use just one balloon and do relay races. This can be competitive – using a stopwatch to time them, or you can let the kids (and yourself) work on their social skills by taking turns.

This game develops gross motor skills, balance, problem solving skills, social interactions and it's fun! Fun is a huge motivator for any child's learning.

4. Tape Jumping

For this game, all you need is some tape! Lay out six to eight strips of tape on the ground about half a metre apart, or closer if needed. This will depend on how far your child can jump. Then let them go for it. Jumping over the tape in any way they like.

You can number the pieces of tape to help keep track, or create games in patterns. As they master the jumping, you can add more for difficulty, or create circuits.

This game fine-tunes the brain as the child learns to jump with two feet together. It also develops balance, gross motor control, feet-eye coordination, and precision and efficacy of movement.

5. Animal Walk Races

Think crab walks, bear walks, penguin walks, bird walks or even the wheelbarrow walk (okay, it may not be an animal, but that's okay).

This can be a quick and easy activity to help your child burn off some energy.

Doing this can provide calming deep pressure to joints, can either burn energy (if completed fast), or slow the body down (if completed in slow motion). It includes role play for the development of imagination and challenges the vestibular and proprioceptive systems.

6. Cardboard Box Hurdles

For this activity, all you need are a few cardboard boxes that the kids can jump over. Set up a row of boxes to hurdle over and let them jump, hop, or skip over the boxes. Very inexpensive, but totally fun!

This game works on both homolateral and cross lateral movements (same side of the body and opposites sides of the body). It develops the efficient movement of individual limbs and develops motor planning abilities. This is how the brain thinks and plans our movement. If you make them large and just a little bit scary, it can also strengthen the ability to take measured risks – essential for all children to learn.

7. Tag

The simple game of tag is a childhood favourite and one that can develop the body and the brain. You can let the children make up their own rules, or you can try freeze tag and have children simply freeze in place until they are set free by the touch of another child.

There are many other variations of the game like requiring tagged children to do a number of star jumps or spins before rejoining the game. It's easy to make this one your own.

Tag teaches your child how to navigate challenges using a little healthy competition. It develops balance, gross motor skills, bilateral movement, and social interactions.

8. Laundry Basket Push

Simply fill a laundry basket up with toys or books or even a small toddler and have your child push it across the room. The heavier it is, obviously, the harder it is for them to push. So, if the basket is too heavy, then encourage your kids to work together to push it. Nothing like sneaking in a little social skills learning through teamwork!

This simple gross motor activity is a great 'heavy work' activity for kids and can be calming for many kids because of the sensory input that it provides. It supports the proprioceptive system, supports contralateral muscle groups, builds muscles and problem solving skills.

9. Hopscotch

Hopscotch is a classic childhood game. Simply draw a hopscotch outline with the numbers 1 – 9 in each square on your driveway with chalk or use tape on the floor inside. Have the children throw a pebble onto the first square, and then jump over it to land in all the other squares, turn at the end and jump back. Repeat this going up all the numbers.

This game is great for working on balance, spatial awareness, fine motor skills and executive functioning (planning the next move). It's also great practice for number recognition!

10. Puddle Jump

Another childhood favourite – jumping in puddles can be extended to include a range of abilities. You don't even need a rainy day to do some puddle jumping. You can use a jump rope and some cups of water. In this game, two people swing an extra-long jump rope, and every other child holds two cups of water while they jump into the rope's jump space. After five jumps, they exit. After each child takes a turn in the jump rope, the one with the most water left in their cups wins. You may want to take this one outside!

Like many of the other games this one is working on all the fundamental building blocks of movement. As we know, movement trains the brain, so the coordination of jumping, holding, thinking, planning, timing, and self-regulation play into the development of the sensory systems and the brain as a whole.

11. What's the Time, Mr Fox?

To play this game, the kids line up a good distance away from the player chosen to be Mr. Fox. The kids shout, "What's the time, Mr. Fox?" And 'Mr. Fox' answers with a time of day. The kids then get to take that number of steps toward him. When the Fox turns around all the children need to freeze. If the Fox sees someone moving, he then sends them back to start again. The first one to touch Mr Fox without getting caught wins, and they become Mr Fox.

You can also try implementing imagination by suggesting Mr Fox describes what kind of steps to take, such as elephant steps or mouse steps. Kids love to pretend to be animals so this will automatically pique the imagination.

When children create and run their own game, they are more intrinsically motivated to participate in it. This goes for all learning – and chores too! Try to give your children choice as much as possible and use these as learning experiences.

This game develops stability, balance, ear/feet coordination, following of instructions, body awareness, and an awareness of force and speed.

12. Rolling

Rolling is so much fun and it's fantastic for the brain. Children can do this on the floor inside or outside. They can do it by themselves, or you can wrap younger children in a blanket and roll them along. They can have their arms by their sides or above their head to protect it.

Rolling helps with the development of your child's brain and body coordination. Rolling horizontally helps assist balance (vestibular system), the proprioceptive system, linear movement awareness, muscle strength and understanding spatial awareness. Once your child has mastered rolling over on a flat surface, take it outside and try rolling down a grass hill. The first one down the hill wins!

13. Tissue Dancing

Have your child start by placing a tissue, light scarf or handkerchief on their heads. Play some music and encourage your child to move about the room - everyone can start dancing. But be careful; don't let the tissue fall off your head! If the tissue hits the ground, you're out, or you can just allow young children to pick it back up and place it on their heads again.

You can extended this game for older children by stopping and starting the music. The kids must freeze in a pose when the music stops.

This is a fun game that works on posture, body control, balance, and concentration.

14. Create

Kids love to create and creating at home is a great opportunity to burn energy and develop their resourcefulness. Give your children a bunch of big empty boxes, paper rolls, and felts – or pencils if you prefer – and leave them to it! If you have old sheets or towels, throw those in too. See what your child comes up with. You can always ask questions or make suggestions if they get stuck, but most children come up with wildly creative contraptions.

This activity develops their problem-solving and planning skills. It develops hand-eye coordination, executive function, imagination, and physical manipulation. It strengthens both fine and gross muscle control and, if done with other children develops communication and collaboration. Plus, they will love explaining to you every little detail of their course.

15. The Floor is Lava

Pull out all of your couch or bed pillows for an easy jumping party! A popular game with children of all ages is 'the floor is lava'. Children can set up a path of cushions and pillows on the floor. Because the floor is now lava they are not able to touch it. They will have to jump from cushion to cushion without falling into the lava! (Ensure any hard furniture or safety hazards are moved away.)

This game is fantastic for gross motor coordination. The ability to plan, execute, control, and evaluate their movement.

16. Soft Toy Throw

Grab a laundry basket or a large bucket or cardboard box can be used. Get your children to choose their favourite soft toys. Then have them throw their teddies into the basket. You can keep score if you want, or challenge them to see how many times they can do it in a row.

You can extend this game by getting them to take a step back each time they successfully get the teddy in the basket.

This game works on hand-eye coordination. The ability of the brain to see an object and then judge how high/low, hard/soft, fast/slow to throw the object. This is also a foundational skill for writing.

Glossary

Altruism: Altruism is defined as a disinterested and selfless concern for the well-being of others. (oxforddictionary.com)

Attachment: is a deep and enduring emotional bond that connects one person to another across time and space (Ainsworth, 1973; Bowlby, 1969). Attachment does not have to be reciprocal. (simplypsychology.org)

Attention Deficit Hyperactivity Disorder (ADHD): A chronic condition including attention difficulty, hyperactivity and impulsiveness. ADHD often begins in childhood and can persist into adulthood. It may contribute to low self-esteem, troubled relationships and difficulty at school or work. Symptoms include limited attention and hyperactivity. Treatments include medication and talk therapy.

Childhood: Childhood encompasses all ages from 0 - 18. Though the latest research indicates that the development of the brain through puberty is not finished until around 24. For the purposes of the philosophies of this book, childhood refers up to the age of 18, where most children would be leaving school.

Empathy: Empathy is the ability to understand and share the feelings of another (oxforddictionary.com)

Exploration: Exploration for the purposes of this book describes an overarching attitude of discovery. It is the freedom to see objects, thoughts and perceptions in new and alternate ways, leading to the exploration of possibilities and the creation and invention of new things.

Fine Motor: Fine motor skill (or dexterity) is the coordination of small muscles, in movements—usually involving the synchronisation of hands and fingers—with the eyes. The complex levels of manual dexterity that humans exhibit can be attributed to and demonstrated in tasks controlled by the nervous system. Fine motor skills aid in the growth of intelligence and develop continuously throughout the stages of human development. (Wikipedia)

Gross Motor: A skill that involves the action of many muscle groups and requires movement of the whole body, e.g. running.

Language: Language here incorporates spoken, unspoken, written and expressive communication. It is the means by which we communicate, and this is most commonly through speech. On a deeper level it also includes body language and attachment. A strong and enduring connection between parent and child.

Lifelong Learning: Lifelong learning is the ability to see the learning process as ongoing throughout the course of one's life. This means it goes beyond school, degrees, awards and achievements. It is an attitude that seeks to learn everything possible from all situations and all people in life. There is always more to learn, always ways to grow.

Love Languages: Gary Chapman formed the love languages theory which surmises that love is received and given in five specific ways. Through touch, gifts, quality time, acts of service and words. It aims to help people to enhance their relationships through quality communication of love.

Metacognition: Metacognition is an awareness or understanding of one's own thinking processes (oxforddictionary.com). Literally thinking about one's own thinking.

Mirroring: Mirroring is the behaviour in which one person subconsciously imitates the gesture, speech pattern, or attitude of another. Mirroring often occurs in social situations, particularly in the company of close friends or family. The concept often affects other individuals' feelings about the individual that is exhibiting mirroring behaviours, which can lead to the individual building rapport with others. (Wikipedia).

Movement: For the purposes that it is discussed in this book, the concept of movement includes any change of position made by the body. Even a subtle shifting of the eyes is considered movement as it is sending information to the brain. It is the premise of the L.O.V.E philosophy that movement is the beginning of all intelligence.

Multiple Intelligences: Howard Gardner is the founder of the theory of multiple intelligences and proposes that there are many forms of intelligence such as kinaesthetic, linguistic, mathematical, spatial etc. Its philosophical basis is that all people are intelligent in different ways.

The Natural Childhood Movement: A philosophy of child development that is centered on the principles of L.O.V.E: Language, Outdoors, Vestibular, And Exploration. This philosophy aims to support children to their fullest potential. It is a movement that incorporates basic principles of living, learning, and communicating. It is centered on age-old traditions and experiences as well as gleaning from modern research and understandings.

Outdoors: This is the natural world. The trees, water, dirt, mountains, forests, deserts and natural environment which surrounds us. It can also include natural and manmade playgrounds, parks and gardens.

Postural Reflexes: The postural reflexes support control of balance, posture and movement in a gravity-based environment. Postural reflex development is mirrored in the infant's increasing ability to control their body, posture and movements.

Primitive Reflexes: Primitive reflexes are automatic stereotyped movements mediated in the brain stem and executed without cortical control (INPP). Simply put, they are movements the brain makes without us thinking about them. They are there as a survival mechanism for our earliest years but need to develop into postural reflexes by four years of age.

Proprioception: Proprioception (or kinaesthesia) is the sense through which we perceive the position and movement of our body, including our sense of equilibrium and balance: senses that depend on the notion of force.

Scaffolding: In education, scaffolding refers to a variety of instructional techniques used to move students progressively toward a deeper understandingm, and ultimately, greater independence in the learning process.

Sensory Processing Disorder (SPD): Sensory Processing Disorder is a condition in which the brain has trouble receiving and responding to information that comes in through the senses. It was formerly referred to as Sensory Integration Dysfunction and is marked by oversensitivity to sensory stimulus such as noise, light and touch (webmd.com).

Sensory Processing System: The Sensory Processing System processes how the brain receives and responds to multiple sensory inputs, such as proprioception, vision, auditory system, tactile, olfactory, vestibular system and taste, and translates them into usable functional outputs. Basically, how our central nervous system processes all the information received through our senses and how we understand that information.

Vestibular: The vestibular system is our primary balance system. It forms in utero (in the womb) and acts as the central balance point for our upright position. The vestibular system is located in our ears and sends and receives messages through the brain to the rest of our body. It undergirds all learning.

References and Further Reading ...

Bauerlein, M. (2009). The dumbest generation: How the digital age stupefies young Americans and jeopardizes our future. Penguin.

Chapman, G., & Campbell, R. (1997). The five love languages of children. Northfield.

Coleman, A. (2008). A Dictionary of Psychology (3 ed.). Oxford University Press.

Connell, G. & McCarthy, C. (2014). A moving child is a learning child: How the body teaches the brain to think. Minneapolis. Free Spirit Publishing.

Costandi, M. (2016). Neuroplasticity. MIT press.

DeLong, R. G. (1993). Effects of nutrition on brain development in humans. American Journal of Clinical Nutrition. 57, 286S-290S

Duckworth, A. (2016). Grit: The power of passion and perseverance. Harper Collins Publishers Ltd.

Dwek, C. (2006). Mindset: How you can fulfil your potential. Ballentine Books.

Goddard, S. (2005). Reflexes, learning and behavior: A window into a child's mind. Fern Ridge Press.

Goddard Blythe, S. (2009). Attention, Balance and Coordination; the A.B.C. of learning success. Wiley-Blackwell.

Goddard Blythe, S. (2011). The genius of natural childhood: Secrets of thriving children. Hawthorne House.

Gottman, J. (2017). The magic relationship ration according to science. https://www.gott man.com/blog/the-magic-relationship-ratio-according-science/

Greenfield, C. (2012). Fostering children's moral and spiritual development in the outdoors [Paper]. Childspace Early Childhood Institute conference.

Harbec, M. (2017). Eating together as a family helps children feel better, physically and mentally. Science Daily. https://www.sciencedaily.com/releases/2017/12/17121409 23 22.htm

Hattie, J. (2018). Updated list of factors related to student achievement. Visible Learning. https://visible-learning.org/hattie-ranking-influences-effect-sizes-learning-achievement/

Konicarova, J., Bob, P., & Raboch, J. (2013). Persisting primitive reflexes in medication-naive girls with attention deficit and hyperactivity disorder. Neuro Psychiatric Disease and Treatment. 9, 1457-1461

Kranowitz, C., & Newman, J. (2010). Growing an in-sync child: simple, fun activities to help every child develop, learn, and grow. Pedigree.

Kvols, K. (1998). Redirecting children's behaviour. Printing Press Inc.

Larkey, S., & Tullemans, A. (n.d.). The ultimate guide to school and home: key strategies for all ages and stages. Sue Larkey Learning Media.

Leaf, C. (2013). Switch on your brain: The key to peak happiness, thinking and health. Baker Books.

Leaf, C. (2019). Think, learn, succeed. Baker Book House.

Levin, A. (2010). My glimpse of hell and the pitiful children who have been betrayed. Retrieved February 2019 from https://www.telegraph.co.uk/news/worldnews/ europe / romania/8128644/My-glimpse-of-hell-and-the-pitiful-children-who-have-been-betrayed.html

McLeod, S. (2009). Attachment. Simply Psychology. https://www.simplypsychology.org/ attachment.html

Miller, D. (2010). Positive Child Guidance (6th Ed.). Wadsworth.

Melillo, R. (2016). The disconnected kids nutrition plan. Tarcher Perigee.

Merga, K. (2017). Research shows the importance of parents reading with children even after children can read. The Conversation. http://theconversation.com/research-shows-the-importance-of-parents-reading-with-children-even-after-children-can-read-82756

Pappas, S. (2012). Early neglect alters kids brains. Live Science. https://www.livescience. com/21778-early-neglect-alters-kids-brains.html

Ratey, J. (2010). Spark. Quercus.

Ratey, J. (2014). Go wild. Little, Brown and Company.

Rayson, H., Bonaiuto, J., Ferrari, P., & Murray, L. (2017). Early maternal mirroring predicts infant motor system activation during facial expression observation. Nature. https://www.nature.com/articles/s41598-017-12097-w

Sandseter, E. (2011). Children's risky play in early childhood education and care. ChildLinks. 3.

Under Wing Therapeutic Services. (2016). Mirroring your child's intense emotions: 4 easy steps. http://www.daniellemaxon.com/blog/2016/4/6/ mirroring-your-childs-intense-emotions

About The Author

Leanne Seniloli works with committed parents and teachers, empowering them to release children's fullest potential. She is the Founder and Director of Without Limits Learning, is a Neuro Developmental Therapist (NDT – INPP), a Senior Lecturer, and a qualified and registered Early Childhood Teacher,  and a Masters student. She has written articles for various magazines and media including 'Early Education', 'The Space', 'Teachers Matter,' 'RadioLive', 'Voxy' and 'The Scoop.'

Leanne has worked with children for over 19 years and has led teams of people to actively engage children in learning. Her own four children have been the inspiration for her commitment to children's development and this combined with extensive study, has ignited her passion to see all children succeed in life and education.

A key driver is to positively impact children's lives so that they can become all they can. Themes of a natural childhood, the outdoors, movement and exploration form the basis of her philosophy as a mother and teacher; and has been the catalyst for the Natural Childhood Movement.

Through her unwavering passion and down-to-earth authenticity, Leanne continues to create programmes, books, and services that provide opportunities for children to have the best life possible. Leanne's programmes, trainings, and lectures will inspire and empower you to release your children's fullest potential.

Visit withoutlimitslearning.com and hashtag #thenaturalchildhoodmovement to join the movement

Additional Programmes by The Author

Simply L.O.V.E. Keep an eye out for future workbooks, workshops and conferences - helping you to create the positive changes you desire for your family.

 Moves 4 me is an individual neuro-developmental therapy programme for your child (incorporating INPP). Visit withoutlimitslearning.com/Moves4Me for more information.

 Moves4LilMinds is the mentoring arm for early childhood centres. Helping teachers assess neuro developmental readiness for learning, implementing the programme and reviewing the results (based on the INPP schools programme).

 Moves4Minds is the mentoring arm for primary schools. Helping teachers assess neuro developmental readiness for learning, implementing the programme, and reviewing the results (based on the INPP schools programme).

 Teachers can be trained over one day to assess neuro motor readiness for learning and implement the INPP programme.

Share your journey at facebook.com/
thenaturalchildhoodmovement

For more ways to connect with the theory,
practice and philosophy of this book, and to
join the community, LIKE Natural Childhood
Movement and Without Limits Learning on
Facebook.

Follow the Without Limits Learning Instagram
page to keep up to date with the latest
initiatives, training, and support.

The Natural Childhood Movement

Use the hashtag
#thenaturalchildhoodmovement when posting
your natural ways of parenting. Share your story,
be inspired, and inspire others!

www.withoutlimitslearning.com

CPSIA information can be obtained
at www.ICGtesting.com
Printed in the USA
BVHW050841291121
622771BV00010B/236